a woman
called

"Our churches are filled with women God has called to lead and preach. They are longing for the blessing of their church families to explore and pursue those roles. Sara's thoughtful, candid and engaging book is a signpost pointing the way towards that journey. Her experience and wisdom serve to encourage women of all ages to find their voices and proclaim the hope of Christ to a world that desperately needs to hear it. As a husband, brother to four sisters and father to three daughters, I'm incredibly thankful for Sara's courage to enter this conversation."

—**Steve Norman**, Lead Pastor, Kensington Church-Troy Campus

"Sara's book is written like a Psalm rather than an epistle. It's lament with hope. It's confessional and personal, not didactic and demanding."

—**Rubel Shelly**, author of *I Knew Jesus before He Was a Christian . . . And I Liked Him Better Then*

"Sara is a compelling storyteller. *A Woman Called* is worth reading for the stories alone. Sara's stories convey truth that must no longer be ignored—that Jesus came to set people free, a freedom for every one of us to live out our calling. Yet as Sara so convincingly reminds us, our freedom in Christ can be hindered by others who also claim to follow Jesus. I applaud Sara for the risks she is taking in honestly sharing her own stories in living out her calling to teach and preach. What she writes is more than worth the freedom it will bring to countless others who will find their own voices echoed in Sara's struggles for freedom and unity in the body of Christ."

—**Mary Albert Darling**, co-author of *The God of Intimacy and Action* and *Connecting Like Jesus,* www.maryalbertdarling.com

"Barton's book is a poignant reminder that 'the women's role issue' is not just about theological positions, but real people seeking to find and fulfill their place in God's kingdom. Agree or disagree with the conclusion, this book elevates the discussion to a deeply spiritual plane."

—**Randy Harris**, author of *Soul Work* and *God Work*

a woman called

PIECING TOGETHER THE MINISTRY PUZZLE

SARA GASTON BARTON

LEAFWOOD
PUBLISHERS

A WOMAN CALLED
Piecing Together the Ministry Puzzle

Copyright 2012 by Sara Gaston Barton

ISBN 978-0-89112-109-1
LCCN 2012009940

Printed in the United States of America

LIBRARY OF CONGRESS CATALOGING-IN-PUBLICATION DATA
Barton, Sara Gaston.
 A woman called : piecing together the ministry puzzle / Sara Gaston Barton.
     p. cm.
 Includes bibliographical references (p.   ).
 ISBN 978-0-89112-109-1
 1. Barton, Sara Gaston. 2. Women in Christianity--United States. 3. Preaching. 4. Women clergy--United States--Biography. 5. Clergy--Appointment, call, and election. I. Title.
 BR1725.B3484A3 2012
 262'.14082--dc23

                                                                    2012009940

Cover design by Elizabeth Fulton
Interior text design by Sandy Armstrong

For information contact:
Leafwood Publishers
1626 Campus Court
Abilene, Texas 79601

1-877-816-4455
www.leafwoodpublishers.com

12 13 14 15 16 17 / 7 6 5 4 3 2 1

For John

To help another person love God is to love another person;
to be helped by another person to love God is to be loved.
—Søren Kierkegaard

Table of Contents

acknowledgments

to Nate: You inspire me to write.

to Brynn: Your faith makes my faith deeper.

to Mark Love: You offered an ideal balance of direct confrontation and a gentle spirit.

to Josh Graves: This book would not exist without your encouragement.

to Andee Cone, Marnie Moore, and Lora Hutson: You gave me courage.

to my share group: Thank you for covering this book with righteous prayer.

to Beth VanRheenen, Phillip Camp, Katie Hays, Greg Taylor, Amy Bost-Henegar, Keith Huey, Rubel Shelly, Naomi Walters, Margaret Blue, Mike Cope, Ken Cukrowski, Randy Harris, Jonathan Storment, Craig Bowman, Josh Ross, and Greg Stevenson: Your careful reading made this a better book, and your time was a gift I will always cherish.

to my editor, Heidi Nobles: I'm grateful God saw fit to pair us for this project.

foreword | by scot mcknight

What you will find in Sara Barton's *A Woman Called* is not an argument, so if you are looking to wrangle with a woman about who should be preaching you might best go elsewhere. What you will find instead of an argument is a story. Scratch that—you will find a life. A life lived under the shadow that instead of breaking the heat actually turns it up. A shadow of mostly men who have taken the Bible seriously, but who even more so have taken their own readings of the Bible so seriously they are no longer open to reviewing the Bible all over again, as if for the first time. I'm convinced it is mostly men who are casting this heat-bearing shadow over women because I, too, was once a shadow-caster. I, too, once thought women weren't called to be preachers.

Until I read the Bible more honestly. I once in a book used the trope of a "blue parakeet," which landed in my yard and oddly taught me how the other birds in the yard behaved, for odd passages in the Bible that don't fit what we believe. Odd passages that make us wonder if our theology is right. Odd passages that, if we but listen to them, we will learn to include and thus read the Bible better. Take, for instance, Deborah, who happened to run Israel from top to bottom. She ran the religious practices, the military machine, and the political show. I never heard about Deborah when I grew up in the church. Take, as another example, Huldah. Some Bible readers don't even know who she is. But she's there, and it was she who was consulted when Josiah wanted to know what to do with this strange book of the Torah discovered in some lockbox in the inner sanctum. Or take Mary, who makes us Protestants break out in a rash just to mention, or Priscilla, who the Bible tells us taught Apollos (it doesn't say she taught only because her husband was present), or take Phoebe . . . or how about Junia, a woman apostle who was called a "prominent apostle." (That's my translation, but it stands with the best scholarship today on the meaning of the Greek.) I never once heard a sermon on those women in the church in which I grew up, and we prided ourselves on being biblical. How can we be biblical if we only talk about the men of the Bible.

These are the "blue parakeet" women in the Bible, and yes there are others—like Ruth and Esther (she saved the whole nation, and we'd all have to admit that's a pretty good life calling). But the Bible lets these blue parakeets sing, and we are silencing them.

Many (again mostly male) leaders today are asking, "What can we let women do in our churches and still be faithful to the Bible?" That's the wrong question. You and I are Bible people. But as Bible people we don't ask that question. We should ask a better one: it's not about what women can do now. The question is this: "What did women do then (in the Bible)?" If you are with me as a Bible person you will say, "Whatever they did in the Bible they can at least do now." If you don't say that you are not truly a Bible person.

But if you are that kind of Bible person, you will let Sara Barton preach in your church. The issue is not if women will preach but will we be faithful to the Bible? The issue here is giftedness. Acts 2 tells us that God would gift women to prophesy, and that means preaching, and the only one stopping them today is (as I say, mostly male) leaders who might be more afraid to let the Spirit do what the Spirit does than to hold onto traditions.

Sara comes from the Churches of Christ, a tradition with roots in the early nineteenth-century Stone-Campbell movement. Churches of Christ stand for preaching, and I have to confess I've heard some of the best preaching in my life among C of C preachers. I think of people like Josh Graves, and Jonathan Storment, and Dave Bland, and I think of the courage of Lee Camp, and the energy of Jerry Rushford, and that Harris fellow down at Abilene Christian, and I think of Mike Cope. Why do you let them preach? Because God's Spirit gifted them to preach. If God were to do the same with women—and he has and he still is gifting women— would you let them preach?

Let the blue parakeets sing if they've a gift for it. Sara's one of them.

introduction | **little story/big story**

Little House on the Prairie was the first story I loved. Created a full one hundred years before my sister Karen and I were born in the 1960s, the Ingalls girls were our "century sisters." For my part, I was enamored with Mary Ingalls. A rule-follower whose hair was always combed neatly, Mary was more to my liking than the messy "little half-pint of sweet cider," Laura. I made believe that I lived in the little house in the woods and the little house on the prairie. One time Karen and I even dressed as Mary and Laura in the Melbourne, Arkansas, Pioneer Day parade. Complete with red, white, and blue pioneer dresses and bonnets hand-sewn by our Nana, we won first place in the children's parade that year. When I read the Little House books, I entered a world of covered wagons and bonnets. But alas, eventually I left. I stopped wearing the costume, and I moved on. It's still fun to go back and visit occasionally, but living on the banks of Plum Creek must come to an end.

I've always loved the idea of entering a story and walking around with the characters. I recall that I could hardly contain my excitement when, as a young girl, I opened a children's book and realized it featured my very own cousin Bryant. His mom, my Aunt Jane, had ordered personalized

books with Bryant's name woven into the storylines. I was mesmerized.
Bryant went on scary adventures with Scooby Doo and Shaggy or peeped
into the trashcan for funny conversations with Oscar the Grouch. I realized that the books were imaginary, but nevertheless I greatly envied the
idea that Bryant was a character in stories that took place in important
places like Sesame Street.

I remember experiencing similar exhilaration in a much deeper
sense as a grown woman when I realized that the Bible offers an invitation to readers to weave our own lives into its plot. When it comes to
Scripture, we are not distant spectators with tiny binoculars who watch
dramatic events from balcony seats high above the stage. The Bible contains ancient history, but it is not purely ancient history. According to
missionary Lesslie Newbigin, the Bible is an interpretation of cosmic history that gives meaning to all human life. That includes Adam and Eve
and Abraham and Jacob and Tamar and David and Jesus and Peter and
Paul and Priscilla and Aquila and you and me.

When we read the Bible, we are invited to embrace a story that claims
to be true, one that interprets all of history in such a way that we must
make a decision: Will we read the story as spectators, as visitors who come
and go just like any other story we might encounter, or will we enter this
story of stories and assume our roles as the people of God in the story
of God?

When I enter books, as I did *Little House on the Prairie*, I forget my
own reality and walk around another place and time. I am entertained
and even enriched by my sojourns. Eventually, however, I leave that world
and return to my real life. I've entered an imaginary world and then left it.
The experience of the Bible, however, is not like that of any other book. It
doesn't fit usual categories: novel, biography, or history. The Bible is not
contained in this temporal world, but it describes a world that we can and
do inhabit. Better yet, the world of the Bible inhabits us. Readers receive

an invitation to reside in the ongoing world presented in the story of Scripture. The Word of God tells a story that is past, present, and future. It's a story that comes from a real past, but we—in the present—are invited to join the story of all eternity. When I realized that my own little life story could be a part of this big story of God, my life gained definition and direction. I was inspired to become part of what God is doing and has been doing for all eternity. I was compelled to join the ongoing plot.

As I stepped into God's story as a young girl and continue to abide there today, I find that it is my calling to teach and preach God's Word in and outside the church. The compelling story of God will not let me go, and I don't want to let go of it. I join my story to God's story. In addition to and woven intricately into the way those stories come together, however, is an additional story, the story of my church tradition. As a woman in my church tradition who discerns a calling to teach and preach God's Word, my narrative does not always fit with the narrative of the church as I know it. And I'm not the only one.

Friends Brad and Jill Cox recently told me about their daughter Maggie. Brad is a minister for their church in Alabama, so the family spends many hours at the church building, where their children play freely. After a recent service, when the crowd had departed, Brad went looking for Maggie and found her in the room behind the pulpit, where baptistery gowns, communion trays, and VBS decorations are kept—you know the one! Maggie had lined up several chairs and was pretending to pass the communion trays at the end of her little row. Brad asked her, "What are you doing, Maggie?" and she replied, "I know I won't ever get to pass the Lord's Supper in church, but I just wanted to see what it feels like."

Maggie wants in on the story. Maggie wants to live and walk and serve in the story, and she already feels left out. It is for the Maggies that I write this book. Abby Smith, a teenager in Missouri, is gifted with singing and songwriting, and she wants to lead worship. It's for the Abbys that I write this book. Poem Harrison, a middle-schooler in Michigan, asked her daddy to build her a lectern. It's for the Poems that I write this book. Amy McLaughlin, a college graduate, has decided to enroll in a master's degree program for religious studies, even though she does not know what the future will hold for her job security. It's for the Amys that I write this book. Our daughters and our sons want to live freely in the story of God. They want to embrace the trajectory we see in the story, that all are one in Christ, and they are ready to live in the fullness of this story here and now, in our day and time.

In my early understanding, the Bible was a static document that I could dissect in order to figure out how to avoid going to hell and secure a place in heaven. But it became the overarching story that gives meaning to my life. Although I will share my story in this book, I hope the compelling story will be not my own but the big one, the one that began in the beginning of all beginnings and gives meaning to all who follow Christ along the way.

> In the beginning was the Word, and the Word was with God and the Word was God. (John 1:1)

part one | **hearing the call**

chapter one | **sara/sarah**

My name is Sara, spelled without an *h*. When I was growing up, I was often asked about the spelling. "Is it spelled like Sarah in the Bible?"

I would answer, "No, I'm Sara without an *h*, so not like Sarah in the Bible."

I read Sarah's name in Scripture, but I have not felt a connection with her any more than I do with Deborah or Bathsheba or any of the Marys. To me, it just isn't the same name. My older brother is a David; he has his connection with the biblical King David. But not me. I have no connection with the biblical Sarah with an *h*, the mother of nations, and don't see how I could. The barrier is far more than the little letter *h*. I don't relate to the nomadic life she lived, the food she ate, the clothes she wore, or the relationship she had with her husband. Because of this background, I was surprised one day when I realized that God was bringing me close to Sarah in the Bible.

It began when I visited St. Stephen's chapel in Mainz, Germany. Its original stained-glass windows were blown out during World War II, and in a stunning tribute to Jewish and Christian reconciliation, the church asked Marc Chagall to design windows that would replace the war-broken ones. The sun shines through the windows and casts the glow of heaven-like blue throughout the chapel. Entering the chapel feels like entering another world. Of all the magnificent windows I have seen in European churches, those are my favorite. Chagall chose to celebrate what Christians and Jews have in common—a love for the Hebrew Scriptures—so the windows are filled with images of the great Hebrew stories.

With the blue glow filling the chapel, I looked around at depictions of the beautiful story of God, and I was drawn to Chagall's tribute to Genesis 18, in which Abraham hosts three visitors. In the stained glass, my eyes initially went to the image of Abraham and the guests around a table. And then I saw Sarah, in the back of the image on the stained-glass pane, peeking out from her place in a nearby tent, leaning closer to hear what the men were saying.

That's me, I thought. That's been my life, leaning and listening, getting as close as I can to the Lord's work in this world, hoping to be invited to the table.

Since experiencing Chagall's Sarah window, I have entered Genesis 18 in new ways. The story of Sarah leaning and listening captivates me. In my mind, I peer over the edge of the basin that was used to wash the visitors' feet, and I see muddy brown water. I hear the noise of the cattle as the servants choose a young calf for the visitors' meal. I smell the yeast in the bread as Sarah kneads dough for the visitors. The scent of smoke from the fire and the aroma of baking bread as it spreads throughout Abraham's homestead pervade my senses. (It seems there's always shared bread in these God stories.) I taste the milk that was served to the visitors; it must have been warm in a desert climate in a pre-refrigerator world. See. Hear. Smell. Taste.

And then, there's touching.

My imagination takes me to Sarah inside her tent, near enough to overhear the conversation between Abraham and the Lord. I imagine how she quieted her nervous breath and leaned toward the sound of their voices, hoping to overhear the words that were spoken. I imagine how her heart must have jumped when she heard her own name and a prophecy about giving birth to a son. I remember the mystery I felt when I found out I was pregnant with my own children. A bit different from Sarah's method of discovery, I looked at the little pink lines on a home pregnancy test, and I reached down and touched my belly in amazement, thunderstruck with the notion that a person was beginning to develop inside me. Sarah must have placed her hands on her old, wrinkled-like-a-raisin belly, and of course her response was laughter.

Sarah's story reminds me of another woman whose womb dried up. When I was living as a missionary in Uganda, I once sat with a woman on a terrible day in her life. This Ugandan woman—I'll call her Alice—had been married to her husband, a good man, for about four years. The first year of their marriage was good, but when there was no baby after one year and then two, the marriage became more difficult.

Women in Uganda (and in reality, women everywhere) are in great part defined by their ability to bear children. In Uganda, a woman's very name changes when her first child is born. For example, I was "Mama Nate" because my firstborn child is Nate. I remember once asking a man his wife's name, and he couldn't recall even though he had been married to her for over twenty years. He and everyone else called her "Mama Fiona" because her firstborn child is Fiona, and through the years her original first name was forgotten.

But Alice was still just Alice. She had no firstborn to define her. If any other name applied to her, it was "poor, barren Alice."

Because she was barren, her husband replaced her and took a second wife. Polygamy is still common in Uganda, and in an act of compassion, Alice's husband did not divorce her (which would have meant a much harder life for her). He promised to provide for her and consider her a wife, but he married another woman to give him children. Alice's womb was seen as replaceable, not only by her husband, but also by most in her community. Even her own parents approved of the arrangement and encouraged her to live peacefully in the marriage. This story is not about being hard on another culture. After all, spouses are replaced for all kinds of abominable reasons in our culture. We even entertain ourselves with stories of polygamous households on reality shows like *Sister Wives*. I don't believe we have any high ground from which to cast our moral stones. Alice's story is about heartbreak, and heartbreak is heartbreak.

So I sat with Alice on a difficult day, the day a marriage celebration took place, bringing a replacement womb into the family. Alice did not attend the celebration, which took place in the village, not far from her house. As we sat in her hut, she prepared tea for me, and we heard the sound of vehicles coming and going as wedding guests arrived. We heard the drumbeats and the shouts of joy as people danced and celebrated.

My experience with Alice helps me further step into the experience of Sarah with an *h*. When we spend time with Sarah, we are invited beyond the senses of seeing, hearing, smelling, tasting, and touching. The invitation is to explore all those times when Sarah was viewed as replaceable—because there were many.

Earlier in the story, as recorded in Genesis 12, Sarah was still young and notably beautiful, and Abraham found himself in danger in Egypt. I imagine that Abraham sat up at night fretting for his own skin, and he hatched a brilliant plan. He decided that Sarah, with her good looks, made a good bargaining chip, so he presented her as his sister and traded her to Pharaoh for some gold and donkeys and sheep.

He replaced the Sarah who slept beside him with a bit of safety to help him sleep through the night.

I wonder how safe Sarah felt on her first night in Pharaoh's harem.

Scripture tells us how God felt about it. God looked down on this agreement and didn't consider it a fair trade. In God's economy, Sarah was *not* replaceable. So God made Pharaoh and his household sick until they saw Sarah *God's* way, and the ailing Pharaoh swiftly gave her back to Abraham, saying, "What have you done to me?" (Gen. 12:18). I'm not so sure Abraham slept very well that night, and yet, he tried the same trick again later, with similar results (Gen. 20).

Now, it wasn't long after the first "she's my sister" incident that I think Sarah herself began to believe she was replaceable. In Genesis 16, Sarah joined Abraham in believing she was interchangeable. She herself must have lain awake at night trying to figure out God's plan for a child for Abraham. Perhaps she put her hands on her aging belly and felt nothing but hopelessness. Devoid of hope, it was Sarah's turn to hatch a brilliant plot to fulfill God's plan for the world.

Sarah decided that her servant Hagar should provide the replacement womb for Abraham's family. This was common custom in ancient culture—as with Ugandan culture—so perhaps everyone thought it was about time for this kind of action. Once the plan was in motion and Hagar gave birth to baby Ishmael, however, Sarah became jealous of her surrogate. I wonder who sat with Sarah on the day when Ishmael's birth was celebrated.

Years passed, and Sarah aged well beyond childbearing years. She was eighty-nine years old when the visitors came to Abraham in Genesis 18.

Sarah did her part in the hosting process. She baked her bread. And now we are back to glimpsing her near the doorway of her tent, leaning, eavesdropping on the conversation among the men. Now we find her laughing as she overhears her own name in the men's discussion.

When Sarah finally gets into the conversation, called out because of her laughter, her instinct is to lie. "I did not laugh," she says. But the Lord disagrees. I like to imagine a moment of humor as the Lord, smiling, says, "Yes, you did laugh."

What fun it would have been to sit with Sarah at the celebration of Isaac's birth. It's recorded in Genesis 21 that on that day, Sarah, who named her child *Laughter*, said "Anyone who hears about this will laugh with me."

When the account of Sarah's laughter is preached, it is often said that the point of the story is God's line in verse 14: "Nothing is too hard for the Lord." That's a good point, and I like it, but there's another point as well, one that connects Sarah's story to the big story of God. See what you think of it: God had a unique place for Abraham and Sarah and Isaac and Jacob and David and the Son of David, and in God's wisdom, Sarah was irreplaceable.

What God has been teaching me through this story of irreplaceable Sarah with an *h* is that God also has a unique place for Sara-without-an-*h*.

I've spent my forty plus years trying to change a clear calling in my life. From the time my parents gave me my name, from the time I first embraced the gospel story, from the times as a teenager when I stayed up late into the night reading and loving God's holy Word, I have been called to teach and preach that Word.

Others have tried to get me to replace that calling. As Sarah did when she took matters into her own hands, I have tried to replace my calling with a different one, one that would make people like me better. In my world, speaking this calling aloud is laughable at the least, blasphemous for some. Many who live outside my world of conservative Christian circles do not understand the magnitude of a woman in my community openly speaking this calling. Trust me, if there were a way around it, I would take an alternate route. There have been moments when I would gladly have traded it for a peaceful night's sleep.

But God says to me, "Sara, I have a unique place to use you, and in my wisdom, you are not replaceable."

Understanding the overarching plot of Scripture, we cannot deny that God stubbornly works in our world through human lives. *We're* not replaceable. This is not some touchy-feely, Hallmark-card "you are special" kind of message from God.

In Scripture, from Genesis to Revelation, God does something that strikes me as illogical. God makes the plot of his story in this world dependent on messy human beings, people who trade their wives for donkeys and sheep, people who laugh out loud at the absurdity of the calling placed upon their lives, people like fishermen and tax collectors and persecutors. God even made redemption for this world dependent on two young kids in a soap opera situation who brought their baby into this world and placed him among smelly farm animals. It's absurd in the plot of early Christianity when the Christian-persecutor, Saul, is called to lead in The Way. It's true throughout the narrative that God's logic defies ours.

God is all powerful, with an ability to snap mighty fingers and part waters. But God chooses to make the plan of redemption vulnerable to us—messy, thoroughly human people. In some mysterious way, God works with people regardless of how obstinate we are, and somehow, redemption comes to miraculous fulfillment both through and despite human beings and the chaos we create.

How does God do it?

It's a mystery. It makes me want to laugh.

Paul explained this mystery with the metaphor of a body:

> Just as a body, though one, has many parts, but all its many parts form one body, so it is with Christ. For we were all baptized by one Spirit so as to form one body—whether Jews or Gentiles, slave or free—and we were all given the

one Spirit to drink. Even so the body is not made up of one
part but of many. (1 Cor. 12:12–14)

Paul taught that each follower contributes to the overall health and function of the body of Christ. I'm not so keen on having any small part of my
body cut off, even a little toe. When I was ten, I lost almost all the vision
in my right eye in a fireworks accident, and my entire body has spent a
lifetime adjusting and compensating for the loss. If I had a penny for every
bruise that came about because of my lack of vision or for every person
with whom I've collided on my right side, I would be rich. Every part
matters in the all-encompassing work of a body, and it's difficult to adjust
to even a minor component that does not function as it was uniquely
designed to contribute in a moving, functioning, breathing, whole body.

In wisdom, and what seems to me at times to be an upside-down way
of thinking, God made redemption of creation vulnerable to his creatures. Could it be that life is about figuring out how we fit into that mysterious, upside-down way of thinking? Sometimes we try to evade God's
plan like Abraham did when he dispatched Sarah to Pharaoh's harem in
exchange for a better night's sleep. Sometimes we try to hurry God's plan
like Sarah did when she sent Hagar to Abraham's tent. Sometimes, like
Sarah, the mother of nations, we have to wait eighty-nine long years to
understand our own place in God's heavenly timetable.

We may laugh at God's gifting for our lives, or as I've learned, others
may laugh at us.

But God says, I have a world to renew, and there's a unique way I want
you to contribute. You might as well face it: I called *you* to be irreplaceable.

✍

chapter two | **leaderette**

When I was a girl, like many kids, I spent quite a bit of my time yearning to be different than I was. Different hair. Different eyes. Different nose. Different hips. Different legs. Different skin. The American obsession with beauty and good looks is widely acknowledged. As a girl, I spent some time wanting to look different, but that wasn't the difference I was *most* concerned about. I wanted a different purpose, a different nature, a difference inside of me. I wanted to trade in something I now understand is related to calling.

Calling is a mysterious and sometimes abused word. When I refer to calling, I understand it to describe the idea that God desires each of us to join the redemption of creation that's been going on since God's good creation was broken and will continue to go on until that redemption is complete as is glimpsed in Revelation. God calls us, not for our own individual benefit, but for a role in the new creation.

For Christians, following Jesus is our primary calling, and then we're given other distinctive personal callings that we are to discern. I don't think calling is some big secret that God keeps hidden from us, but neither is it tattooed on our foreheads when we're born or written in the sky after baptism. God reveals calling to us, not as individuals set apart from Christian kinship, but found in connection with community and immersion in Scripture. For we are God's handiwork, created in Christ Jesus to do good works, which God prepared in advance for us to do (Eph. 2:10).

God gives believers a calling related to their contribution to new creation, and discerning that calling is central to following the way of Christ. It involves a combination of opportunities and open doors, unique gifts, talents, and personalities. Scripture teaches us that the process of being called is mysterious and even mind boggling. At times God clearly calls people despite an obvious lack of talent. Moses, who described himself as slow of speech and lacking eloquence, was called as a mouthpiece to Pharaoh. Deborah, a female prophet, was called among warriors. David, the eighth of the eight sons of Jesse, literally the least expected, was God's chosen. Matthew, a mistrusted tax collector, was called as one of the twelve. Calling pushes against our own desires and that which gives us immediate joy and fulfillment. Jeremiah, Elijah, Esther, and Peter weren't overjoyed when they were called, so I am certainly not alone in my wrestling match with calling.

Joan Chittister describes the mysterious process of calling in *Heart of Flesh.*

> If God is anywhere, the greatest writers of the spiritual life
> have taught for centuries, God is in us, bringing us to life,
> drawing us incessantly on to that place where we become
> everything we can be. The soul, that place where the human
> meets the divine, lives to develop the God-life in us here and
> now, to be light whatever the darkness that surrounds us, to
> bring us to a sense of self that satisfies without subsuming
> everything else in its path. The posture of the soul before
> a God who dwells in the heart of us to give us life, to give

us peace, to give us security, is at once a profound bow and
at the same time a wide-open embrace of the universe. It is
a mix of audacious humility and diffident pride that gives
the lie to everything we've ever been told to the contrary
about both.

As a girl, I could not have articulated calling as a simultaneous "profound
bow" and "open embrace." But, as I look back on life, I know God was
teaching me to listen for my calling: to love God and love others uniquely.
It's been like a thirst that cannot be quenched. I simply must discern how
I may contribute to God's work in new creation. It's when I live into calling
that I find the blessing, joy, peace, and fulfillment our world longs for.

As I sought to discern how I might contribute through a unique calling, I was drawn to options other than what seemed to be expected of me.
In general, the message I perceived was that women, in particular, should
not seek certain types of attention. It seemed to me that a girl might seek
attention related to external looks and beauty, but she must be quite careful in bringing attention to internal thoughts and ideas, especially if she
had strong opinions about politics, society, or church. This was solidified
by what I saw when I looked around at significant ways women might be
noticed and applauded in society.

Beauty contests, the most obvious way girls took center stage, started
in my community with baby girls as young as two years old. The pageants did not involve talent competitions or interviews; they were based
exclusively on outer appearance. I was in a few of those beauty pageants
as a teenager. I remember the feeling of standing in the middle of a stage,
lights illuminating the frilly green pageant dress I had borrowed from
my cousin, Carla, while judges took notes on me. I smiled until my cheeks
hurt, holding a cardboard and glitter number at just the right height
in front of myself. This all made sense in my world. I wanted to fit my

culture's definition of a lady, but I perceived that I fell short of that definition, and I didn't like it. I never won a beauty contest, by the way.

Now I have a daughter, and I desperately want Brynn to explore her calling, not some cardboard and glitter concoction of who our culture says she should be. I want her to possess a strong sense of identity as a human being, which I believe is ultimately found in recognizing herself as a woman, made in God's own image with a distinctive calling to contribute to others. Henri Nouwen writes in his book *Life of the Beloved* about finding identity in one's "belovedness" and knowing that God sees each unique one of us as *beloved*. That's what I want for both of my children, that each of them will find identity in being valued by God. I want them to know that in God's holy presence, they enter the only stage that matters and stand before the Judge whose notepad says, "By all my calculations, as I gaze at you, my beautiful child, you are beloved."

Living into God's purpose, however, is not left to an individual's discretion. It doesn't come as an optional feature in human beings, the way that sunroofs and heated seats are optional in automobiles. Understanding our identity as a called person is not like buying an external product to install like a remote starter on a car. Understanding calling is internal. It's complicated, and it's hard won. Like many of us insecure human beings, my internal struggle to discern calling involved wanting to please others with my life more than I wanted to please God. I had little success in my young venture to be someone I was not—little success in trying to install a calling that did not come inside me.

I was born and raised in a small town in a southern Bible-belt church in Arkansas. When I was a teenager, my congregation began to participate in a nationwide program that trained young people for church leadership. Jack Zorn, a church leader from Alabama, wanted to teach young men to lead, and in 1969, he started a program he called "Lads to Leaders."

The program taught young men to give speeches, read and memorize Scripture, and speak public prayers, all noble and worthwhile ventures.

The program was expanded to include girls in 1974, but it was important to churches in our tradition to distinguish between the leadership of young males and young females. Jack Zorn invented an interesting word to solve the dilemma; he called the girls' portion of the program "Lasses to Leaderettes." So, in the 1980s, I entered the program as a young leaderette.

It was widely accepted in my tradition that Christians shouldn't expect the same kind of leadership from young lasses as from young lads. In response to questions as to whether the Leaderettes program trained female preachers or song leaders, the official statement from Lads to Leaders was found in my red Leaderette training folder (the folder had a big swirly L on it—I thought it looked just like the one on Laverne's shirt in the old TV show *Laverne and Shirley)*: "Training girls is very important. Females are in the majority in many churches. They are needed as Sunday school teachers, in VBS, and teaching women's classes. They need to be equipped to teach others the gospel. 1 Corinthians 14:34 restricts the role of women in the church. Girls give speeches and lead songs only with other women present."

As a young woman, fair or not, I understood that to mean men do not need women when it comes to spiritual matters, and I internalized that women are not needed by God as much as men. My experience as a basketball player provided an apt metaphor: Women are inherently second-string players who will never get into a real game. Perhaps my teenage mind was not fair regarding the program's interpretation of Scripture, but I was compelled to try to make sense of what I was taught by my community and how it intersected with the calling the Holy Spirit was articulating within me.

This word "leaderette" and the interpretation of Scripture it represented to me describe how I have felt about my thoughts and opinions.

"-Ette" them. Minimize them. Contain them. Lady-like them. But I joined the program nonetheless, and I came alive when I read Scripture and presented my understandings to others. I loved the experience. Maybe it's a really geeky thing for a teenager to enjoy, but it shouldn't be. Until that point, I had not experienced something that connected with my inner thirst as this experience did. As I began to succeed in teaching Scripture in this program, I felt confused and vulnerable, like a young tree, bracing itself for an approaching Arkansas tornado.

I sensed that storm brewing for a long time. When the storm came, it didn't come as an Arkansas tornado but as a Kenyan monsoon in my own spirit. While in college, I went to Kenya for a mission internship. The trip blew me in a whole new direction. While I was in Kenya with a group of six other students from Harding University, we stayed with a missionary family: Monte and Beth Cox and their three children. Monte is a natural-born visionary. He lives to mentor people. He's convinced hundreds of people to sell everything they own, say goodbye to their families, and move to Africa. Admittedly, God and Beth help him do that, but he has that kind of influence.

When we were in Kenya, as well as Kenya's neighboring country, Uganda, Monte taught us about being a team, working together for God's purposes, and using our gifts for the world rather than for ourselves. Monte led us in thinking about calling.

Early in our experience, Monte gave our group an assignment. He told us that while we were in Kenya, we would be asked to present programs for young people in village church communities, so he encouraged us to devise a strategy for what we would do in these programs. He told us to take about an hour to agree upon a plan, so we all started throwing around ideas. Susan Vaughn was the idea person. She threw out about ten ideas in the first five minutes. Her brother David was more practical. It was his sister we were dealing with, so he disparaged a few of her ideas and shared why they would not work. Jenna, a cheerleader at Harding, played that same role in our group, praising Susan for her ideas and David for his practicality. Then there was me. I took a look at my watch, mentally noting that fourteen valuable minutes had already been "wasted." I got out a piece of paper and mapped out a plan for what we would do when we were in the villages and assigned jobs to each of my teammates. When I got a moment, I took over the conversation and presented them with the idea. Monte didn't enter the conversation.

Unbeknownst to us, as we spent this hour in discussion, Monte pretended to be disinterested in our conversation while he was actually sitting in the corner, taking notes about our group and our temperaments. When we completed our task, with four minutes to spare (thank you very much!), Monte revealed to us that the exercise was not chiefly about what we would do when we went to the Kenyan villages. He used the exercise to get us to think about our ability to function as a team. He then distributed information about temperament types. He was keen on a book by Tim LaHaye called *The Spirit-Controlled Temperament*, about four basic types of human temperament and how all types contribute to healthy functioning of the whole.

Monte shared that he wasn't sure about all of us, but he thought Susan was sanguine and that I was choleric. Monte shared that he had noticed how I had taken over the situation and controlled the conversation; he pointed out that perhaps I had sidetracked some creativity the others were bringing to the conversation in my quest to accomplish the task quickly and within the given time frame. Monte said he was actually surprised that the group went with my plan, since it wasn't one of the best ideas presented, although it was quite practical.

Feeling a bit insulted, I quickly perused the information Monte gave us. As I read about my identified persona (or shall I say nemesis), "Cathy Choleric," I immediately knew that I did not like her very much:

> The Choleric is the no-nonsense person—practicality is
> her way of life. Self-sufficient, active, and hard-working,
> the Choleric gets it done. . . . The Choleric plans quickly,
> almost intuitively sizing up what needs to be done, then fol-
> lows the plan. You won't catch her deliberating too long over
> details. This dogmatic person is a born leader, very keen,
> and capable of responsibility. She will take a stand and stick
> to it, no matter what—a good and bad aspect, as she will not
> be influenced by what others think, but of the four tempera-
> ments, she is also the least sensitive or sympathizing with
> others. You learn to steer clear of Cathy Choleric if you want
> a shoulder to cry on—she'll just diagnose your problem and
> give you a solution. But if you understand her personality,
> you'll find her fun to be around and very capable.

I was not happy *at all* with my temperament type.

I did not want it.

I wanted to be like Susan, whose temperament was described with
words like *warm, caring, sincere,* and *loving.* Everyone liked Susan, and *sanguine* was just a more appealing word than *choleric,* which sounded like
a cuss word to me. Susan, the president of the student body at Harding
University, was a leader and likeable at the same time. Monte told me that
Brent Abney, a friend of mine, was also a choleric, and that really didn't
help things much. I remember thinking that it made sense for Brent to be
choleric. After all, Brent was a man! He was supposed to be decisive and
dogmatic and capable and a leader. I was a woman. I was supposed to be
soft and silent and a follower. I found great dissonance in exploring how
one could be both a lovable woman *and* choleric.

My time in East Africa was a defining moment in my search for
who God created me to be. I cried real tears and mourned my choleric

temperament for hours on end during our long four-wheel-drive adventures through the potholes of Uganda and Kenya. I was so thankful that my best friend Marnie was on the trip, because I knew that Marnie loved me even before my flaws (as I saw them) were revealed for all to see. However, after that personal personality storm, I understood my calling better, despite its dissonance in my world. I withstood the storm that called an aspect of my nature by name. After that, I began the long process of making peace with who God was calling me to be and figuring out how that person fit into my church and family and society.

Through this process of naming my temperament type, along with exposure to a world much wider than my upbringing, God helped me embrace my belovedness. It was as if God reached out with big, heavenly hands and put a pair of glasses over my eyes so that I could see who I was meant to be and could stop trying to be someone else. It was then that I realized I was God's beloved child, called for a purpose beyond myself.

I heard the call to be a missionary to Uganda while I was on that trip in East Africa. We spent our time mostly in Kenya, but we took an extended trip to nearby Uganda. At that time, Uganda was coming out of a long period of civil strife, dating back to the infamous Idi Amin. The country had been closed to residence by foreigners but was re-opening, and Monte Cox and his teammate, Kevin Kehl, challenged our group to consider moving to Uganda and being a part of the healing that was already taking place there. We couldn't help but notice how Uganda's structures were seriously broken. The roads, built to be smooth surfaces of asphalt and concrete, had been neglected for several decades and were comprised of one pothole crater after another. Bombed-out army tanks along the roadside were evidence of the violence that preceded us. We carried our own containers of fuel as we traveled because many of the fuel stations did not consistently have diesel, and we went through army roadblocks armed by teenagers with AK-47s. We drove through Queen

Elizabeth Game Park, where Uganda's wildlife had suffered for decades during the war and was coming back to life, like the black plains of grass we drove through after a fire, ready for fresh, new, hopeful birth.

On that short trip, I came to love Ugandan people, Ugandan history, and the Ugandan soil itself. I remember the very moment when I was leaving Africa aboard a cigarette-smoke filled Alitalia plane, and as the wheels of the plane rose and I lost physical connection to the continent, I knew I would be back and that there was a role that fit my calling. Can God use airplane wheels to call us? It seems to me that God spoke through Balaam's donkey, and airplanes are just a newer form of transportation. It was in that precious moment that I began to see my life through newly focused lenses as the kind of person who could be used by God—a strong disciple with a calling, a temperament with a purpose, a woman with hands and feet that the Spirit was priming to be used in a hurting world that needs compassionate people. I began to see myself as a woman with just enough understanding of her unique calling to go where God was leading.

As I write about calling, I draw from various experiences: my birth in 1968 during the height of social upheaval in the United States, my upbringing in a small town in Arkansas, my cultural perception as influenced by eight years in a developing country, my experience as a partner in a wonderful marriage of mutual submission to each other, and my years of immersion in academic environments that encourage open exploration of ideas, especially within the areas of religion and spirituality. I don't speak for all women. I am just one woman who has seriously contemplated Scripture's guidance in regard to my spiritual life and calling as a part of Christ's body and in service to the world. That's the call for all Christians, so I am not unique. All Christians are to be about the business of contemplating the grand story of Scripture as it intersects with our own experiences of human life in our own times and places. We're all supposed to bow to God and embrace the universe simultaneously.

It seems to me that in human relationships, as we all search for our own unique identity, we encounter situations in which our search feels more like a collision than an embrace; hugs just get awkward sometimes when two parties don't come at it in unison. Martin Luther King Jr.'s *Letter from a Birmingham Jail* contains a line that reads, "We are all caught in an inescapable network of mutuality." So while we each search for our individual and unique calling from God, the Christian life is not just about the individual. The inside of me is connected to the inside of my family and friends. I cannot escape how my story is not merely *my* story, but it is a story of *us*, of human beings in inescapable relationship with each other. As we each listen for our calling, we help others listen as well. We cannot escape that process if it is as God designed it to be.

The body of Christ, which is the context of my discussion about gender roles, is innately a unit of deeply connected people living in "inescapable mutuality." Ideally, as one person finds his or her identity in Christ, others are uplifted, made stronger, and encouraged to find identity for themselves. Unfortunately, this is a broken world in which relationships are not as God originally intended them to be, and as we wrestle with the effects of brokenness, we hurt one another. I have often wondered whether the ultimate purpose of life is for us to learn to love one another in the manner that Jesus, perfect in the image of God, modeled love. The aspect I most anticipate about heaven is not the golden streets or the pearly gates, but the true, right, and pure connection in community with the Father, the Son, the Spirit, and fellow human beings. I can't wait for the day when we all see each other as God sees us, our vision restored to 20/20 when it comes to truly setting focused eyes upon one another.

Until that time in heaven, however, a story like mine will cause conflicting reactions. When some women hear me speak about gender roles in church ministries, they feel validated. They are thankful that I'm saying it. They tell me so.

Other women, however, feel anything but validated. The story wounds them.

Sometimes, to my dismay, women react to my desire for a redefinition of women's roles in ministry not by feeling validated but by feeling vulnerable. My calling to a public teaching role sometimes causes other women to feel that their gifts are not valued. They are gifted and fulfilled in traditional roles among one another and children, and I sometimes make them feel that I am looking down my nose at their contributions. It hurts me to know that I sometimes cause these wounds, even within my own family and congregation and college ministry work. It seems so very wrong that in one person's desire to function as God created her to function in the body, she might cause another woman to feel discounted in her function. I long for a community in which every part of the body uses the gifts they've been given by the Spirit, roles not pitted against each other but connected to one another. Going back to Paul's description of the church body:

> Now if the foot should say, "Because I am not a hand, I do not belong to the body," it would not for that reason stop being part of the body. . . . If the whole body were an eye, where would the sense of hearing be? If the whole body were an ear, where would the sense of smell be? But in fact God has placed the parts in the body, every one of them, just as he wanted them to be. If they were all one part, where would the body be? As it is, there are many parts, but one body. The eye cannot say to the hand, "I don't need you!" And the head cannot say to the feet, "I don't need you!" On the contrary, those parts of the body that seem to be weaker are indispensable, and the parts that we think are less honorable we treat with special honor. And the parts that are

unpresentable are treated with special modesty, while our presentable parts need no special treatment. But God has put the body together, giving greater honor to the parts that lacked it, so that there should be no division in the body, but that its parts should have equal concern for each other. If one part suffers, every part suffers with it; if one part is honored, every part rejoices with it. (1 Cor. 12:15, 17–26)

I don't know many Christians who would say that they spend a great amount of time rejoicing with all the parts of the body because they are all working in unselfish tandem like a human body works.

It is socially acceptable that intelligent, professional adults spend hours and hours in therapy trying to figure out who they are and how their childhood family experiences have complicated their identities. If we're living authentic church family life, it stands to reason that we'll all experience something similar as we deal with the complicated relationships of church family. When we live *body life*, church life, in a broken world, things are going to be complicated. When it comes to following Jesus, I don't think we were promised a rose garden but something more like Gethsemane.

Since I was a little girl, I have taken the call to body life seriously. I have tried to find my place in the body and to figure out my function. I did not *desire* the gifts I seem to have been given, teaching and preaching. They are gifts, however, and there's a certain humility in accepting the gifts we're given.

When our daughter Brynn was young, she once made a faux pas as she was given a gift. Our friends, Mike and Diane Cope and their sons Chris and Matt, visited our family in Uganda while we lived there. Brynn was about five at the time. We eagerly awaited visitors when they came, and for a five-year-old girl, a large part of the excitement was opening the presents that inevitably came out of the suitcases from the other side of the world. The Copes brought Brynn a doll, a reasonable gift for a five-year-old girl. When they gave it to her, Brynn eagerly opened the package, but then with a disappointed, straightforward confession, she handed the doll to Diane and said, "I'm not really in to dolls. Did you bring me anything else?"

That's how I felt about my gifts at times during the discernment process. Could I just look at God and say, "Did you bring me anything else?" My life would be a great deal easier if I could just choose my own gifts. I have desired gifts that make sense in my world, gifts that my social realm says are appropriate for women, gifts that are affirmed, understood, and appreciated. I have tried to be a part of the body I was not called to be. But no matter how hard one tries, it's not possible to turn an ear into an elbow.

I know my gifts are not the most important gifts, and I recognize that my faith does not stand or fall if they go unused. I know men who sense the call to preach or teach, and yet for one reason or another they do not feel welcome to use their gifts in their own churches. They have body image issues as well.

As I wrestle, I note that Paul writes later in chapter 12, "Now, eagerly desire the greater gifts." And, he goes on to clarify with his most excellent words in 1 Corinthians 13 that love is the greatest gift of all. As we read about the worship confusion of Corinth, we see that love is both the solution and the goal. Paul reminds me that Jesus calls me, despite any confusion over gifts and roles and the body of Christ, to live in submissive love toward the members of the body of Christ.

Love is a radical call.

It's a call that sounds so very un-American, to put my own individual desires and gifts aside until the other members of my church body desire me to use them in their midst (and possibly never use them). In a patient process of discernment with my local congregation, I must decide if I can be true to my calling if the situation stays the same.

In Paul's description of the body, all parts of the body are interdependent. All parts are needed. There is no inferiority in gifts that are not immediately visible, and there is no superiority in gifts that are center stage. If I could wish one heavenly reality into our earthly lives, it would be that we would honor one another equally as we rejoice in whatever gifts we've received.

What would happen if we found our calling in Christ, explored our unique gifts in the body of Christ, and actually rejoiced with one another in those gifts as Paul describes? I think that sometimes we're so worried about sounding prideful that we don't rejoice in any gifts. We downplay the language of gifting because we fear someone else might think we are full of ourselves. Or we fear making it seem that some gifts are better than others.

In *The Screwtape Letters* by C. S. Lewis, a demon writes to his understudy about how our understanding of talents and character may be convoluted:

> . . . The most alarming thing in your last account of the patient is that he is making none of those confident resolutions which marked his original conversion. . . . I see only one thing to do at the moment. Your patient has become humble; have you drawn his attention to the fact? . . . Catch him at the moment when he is really poor in Spirit and smuggle into his mind the gratifying reflection, "By Jove! I'm being humble," and almost immediately pride—pride at his own humility—will appear . . . You must therefore conceal from the patient the true end of humility. Let him think of it not as self-forgetfulness but as a certain kind of

opinion (namely, a low opinion) of his own talents and character. . . . By this method thousands of humans have been brought to think that humility means pretty women trying to believe they are ugly and clever men trying to believe they are fools . . . and we have the chance of keeping their minds endlessly revolving on themselves in an effort to achieve the impossible.

Imagine the difference we could make in one another's lives and in the life of the world if we actually functioned as a body, if we rejoiced with humility with one another in our gifts, and if love actually won in our lives as it wins in 1 Corinthians.

I've been preaching occasionally at the Central Woodward Christian Church, which is not far from my home congregation, the Rochester Church of Christ. I fill in as a guest when their pastor is out of town. This congregation is what we call a cousin church to my own church. Our churches are similar in numerous aspects of our theology and practice. When I walked into their building and saw a portrait of Alexander Campbell, a forefather in our church movements, I felt right at home.

Although we share a common heritage, several aspects of our worship practice differ, the role of women in church leadership being one dramatic difference. In the congregation to which I belong, we are in a time in our congregational history in which women are doing more than in the past, although there is still clear delineation between the roles of men and women. We have varying rules about women for our different services as well as a public statement that women will never serve as the pulpit minister or an elder at the church. At Central Woodward Christian, however, women are fully included in leadership, and the congregation has women and men who serve as pastors, preachers, worship leaders, and elders.

The first time I stood to preach to that group of about a hundred people, mostly with gray hair, I felt peace. On the rare occasions when I've preached in my own congregation, it has been a team-preaching situation, accompanied by a man. Even in those situations in which male authority was made clear to the congregation, I knew some people in the congregation were upset and uncomfortable, no matter how I did it, what I said, or who was in charge. But when I stood in front of this little group at Central Woodward Christian, that tension was absent. I opened Scripture, and I preached. It wasn't spectacular. It was just a regular sermon. They use a lectionary to guide worship each week, so I didn't even choose a text with which I thought I could especially impress anyone. After contemplating God's Word on behalf of a group of Christians in preparation for the sermon, I preached as the Spirit guided me. It was a significant moment in my life when I used my gifts for the benefit of the church, and I felt joy in it. They encouraged me. No eye in this body was saying, "I don't need you," and no ear was saying, "I don't want to hear you."

I wish I could write that when I preached at Central Woodward Christian, I felt "complete" joy in it, but that would not be true. When I preach as a guest in this nearby congregation, I miss out on what's happening across town at my own congregation. That makes me sad and steals a bit of the joy.

I've been asked why I don't leave my faith heritage and join a different one that already welcomes leadership of women—why not just join the Central Woodward Christian Church?

The answer is, I don't want to leave my own group and join another one. I know every body of Christ encounters difficulty when it comes to each member of the body embracing his or her calling. No group of people is perfect. On this side of heaven, beloved identity in human beings will not be fully understood or wholly experienced.

One's place in a unit is hard to embrace. Some people leave their biological families of origin for good reason because of pain they experienced in the family unit, and they sometimes find joy outside that family. I would say that most people I know in that situation, however, also have a deep sense of sadness regarding family life.

If I left my church heritage, I would feel deep sadness. I believe that if I were to say, "I am not a part of this body," I would not for that reason cease to be part of it. Churches of Christ have raised me and loved me and given me my primary calling as a follower of Christ. The rest is complicated, and I expect it will continue to be until Jesus heals his broken body once and for all.

chapter three | **a blank piece of paper**

I have this friend, Katy, who gets freaked out by empty paper and writing assignments. She procrastinates and worries and can't get started. I once forced her to write a paper about herself to send along with her application for admission into a master's degree program. Once she got started, she wrote a fine paper. She's not a *bad* writer at all, just a resistant writer. She's my stick-shift friend (we both prefer to drive cars with a stick shift), and sometimes I imagine her writing process like a stick-shift car that is stalled and needs a push to get going. Once you give her a push, she knows the timing of the clutch, she shifts at the right time, and she becomes confident. She's fine once someone pushes her to get started.

I, on the other hand, love a blank piece of paper. I prefer lined paper, perhaps because I'm a writer and not an artist. But, really, any kind of paper will do, and the paper calls out for words. For me, it's as if the paper offers an invitation, and I get to decide if I will RSVP. A brand new blank journal or a blank document on my computer screen elicits the same kind of reaction.

I have never had writer's block. I look at paper or at the computer, and I can think of *something* to say. I have written countless drafts that were destined for the trashcan, but on almost any day, at any time, I can sit down and write *something*. I don't really have much patience with students who can't think of something to write. Writing possibilities, whether they are good or not, are "to infinity and beyond," as my son used to quote when he was four and learned about infinity from Buzz Lightyear. I love a blank piece of paper.

And yet, a few years ago, a question about a blank piece of paper made me feel hopeless and angry. Let me explain.

The congregation I attend had been looking for a children's minister for almost two years, and a situation had not yet worked out. That seemed like a long time, and somewhere in the search, I started wondering if maybe I should apply for the job. I have always wanted to work for a church, and it didn't seem likely to me that I would get a chance to work for a church unless I worked in children's ministry. This is the one area in Churches of Christ that is most open to a woman who wants to work in ministry. Sometimes we play with semantics to avoid tension. We might call the children's minister the "children's education coordinator" or the "Sunday school director." Avoiding the word "minister" and the name of a woman existing on the same line of the church bulletin will head off some tension. There's a hesitancy to call a woman a minister, even if she is one. But my congregation was looking for a minister *and* calling the position *Minister for Families with Children* in order to denote that she or he would minister to all the families in this life stage, a minister to the children and their parents. That sounded appealing to me.

In some ways, I am very good with children. I love being a mother. I loved teaching my children the alphabet and colors and animals and books of the Bible. Books are a central part of our family life; reading brings us together. We're Harry Potter people and Narnia people and Dr. Seuss people and, well, book people. I love to take education and connect it to spiritual life. My kids know that a conversation about raking leaves will not remain a conversation about leaves for long. We'll eventually talk about the connection between leaves and the spiritual life. My kids know that an activity such as baking will not remain an activity merely about baking. We'll eventually talk about the connection between eating and God. I began to think that maybe what I did with my own children and their spiritual formation could be a path for what I could do with children and families at church.

In my most honest moments, however, I had to admit that the part about working with the parents of the children was more exciting to me than the part about working with the children themselves. When I think of my teaching gifts, I realize that they are more apparent when I teach adults than when I teach children.

Regardless, I wanted to work for a church enough that I was willing to give it a chance. There are few ministry opportunities that come along for women and few women in ministry who really find the job of their dreams. It's a small niche that requires a great amount of adaptation.

At first, Josh, who was working on the staff at the church, was very supportive of my interest in this position. He encouraged me to apply. We had worked together in college ministry for a few years, and I thought Josh had a good idea of my abilities in ministry.

I decided to apply for the job and see what would happen. The process was long, and during these months, I began to notice that Josh seemed to change his mind about me fitting this job. It puzzled me a bit because he had been so supportive at first. But I also understood what he understood, that it was becoming more and more apparent that I was trying to fit a square peg into a round hole; my calling in life was square, and the hole for children's ministry was round. I was not cut out for children's ministry in the way that the job would need to be done in this situation, and I was beginning to see this, as were others in the decision-making process.

It was hard for me to let go of the idea, though, because I thought this might be my only chance to work for a church. I was willing to deny my square-peggedness and try to be a round peg if a round peg was needed. Ultimately, the church leaders offered me a different part-time job instead of the children's ministry job, and I accepted their offer to work as a part-time small-groups minister for a stint. I appreciated their desire to adapt with me, but a part-time job in addition to my full-time job as a campus minister did not ultimately prove to be manageable, so I didn't sign on for another term after the first year.

Josh and I had several conversations about my life and ministry during this time, and one conversation still stands out. Josh asked me, "Sara, if you had a blank piece of paper, what would you do with your life?"

I immediately began to cry. His question made me furious and sad and hopeless all at the same time. I said, through my tears, "You may be able to imagine a blank piece of paper, but I can't. I've never had a blank piece of paper, and I never will."

Josh wished he hadn't asked me that question.

Josh's question was a good question. I shouldn't have reacted with anger and frustration. But I did, because in my entire life, no one else had thought to ask me that question. When it was asked, as it should have been, I didn't even know how to answer. The question addressed calling, a word I had heard male preachers use to describe why they preach, an experience that was off limits for women.

Really, it's an illusion that any of us have a blank piece of paper in life. We like to think that we can do and be anything we want to be, but life has a way of making a few scribbles on our papers even when we don't want them there. Almost all people struggle to find the right words for the paper of their lives. Many seem to have writer's block when it's time to make vocational decisions, and many lack the innate skills required for the career they want to pursue. Some students make the wrong decision about what to study in college and end up in a career that isn't what they really want. Like Katy's writer's block, some people need a little push to get going in life's calling, and then they fly.

I realize that I am not unique in my struggle to write the story of my life. But it does create a challenge when you have your paper all sketched out and ready to go, and you find that others have already written your story for you with a character in your story who looks nothing like you.

What do you do when you try to write your life and someone else comes in with a red pen and gives you a zero? What do you do when you try to write your life and someone takes your paper, crumples it, and tosses it in the trash?

I believe that true writers write for themselves, not for others. They write because they have to, because they will go crazy if they don't, and because there's an insatiable thirst to put pen to paper. Writers realize that no one may want to read what they've written. My own writing was not initially conceived for publication, and without Josh's insistence, it wouldn't be in publication. My writing exists because it must exist. In the story of my life, there was nowhere else for these thoughts to go. If someone wants to read what I've written, I'll say, "Thanks for reading my piece of paper."

One's calling, however, cannot be crumpled up and thrown away. One's vocation is not an assignment to be graded with a red pen. One's spiritual gifting from God is not optional for publication. In Christianity, each life gift is to be published. It is to be used. It is to exist. Until Christ returns, this is a broken world, and life doesn't always work out even when it comes to spiritual calling. Nevertheless, it's our responsibility as Christians to discern our gifts and use them for the benefit of others. We are not whole when we do not. We are an incomplete book with several pertinent chapters violently ripped from the binding. We're meant to join the whole story:

> Now to each one the manifestation of the Spirit is given for the common good. To one there is given through the Spirit a message of wisdom, to another a message of knowledge by means of the same Spirit, to another faith by the same Spirit, to another gifts of healing by that one Spirit, to another miraculous powers, to another prophecy, to another distinguishing between spirits, to another speaking in different kinds of tongues, and to still another the interpretation of tongues. All these are the work of one and the same Spirit, and he gives them to each one, just as he determines. (1 Cor. 12:7–11)

Josh is the best kind of friend, and he's still asking me questions about calling, and I'm still trying to answer him. Ultimately, I'm still trying to answer God. I'm still seeking to discern the mysterious work of the Spirit who distributes these gifts. God has given me a piece of paper, and I want to write and live a story that honors what I've been given. It was out of that conversation that I began to scribble on my own paper with my own handwriting. It was then that I overtly put my calling and the word "preaching" together in the same sentence.

Living in East Africa for several years taught me how American and individualistic it is to think we have exclusive rights to our stories. I can imagine a Ugandan brother or sister reminding me that we are co-writing with God, who is in control, and with our communities, who write alongside us. Bernhard Anderson, in his book *The Unfolding Drama of the Bible*, helps me to think about how I'm ultimately writing and living my little story in community and as part of God's ongoing action. He explains that, when we encounter the Bible:

> We are not to be spectators of something that happened once upon a time. The Bible is not a book of ancient history.

It is more like commedia dell-arte, a dramatic form that flourished in sixteenth-century Italy. To be sure, it was not a free improvisation, for there were some given elements: There was a director, there was a company of actors, and there was a story plot that was given to them in broad outline. With these given elements they were told to improvise—that is, to fill in the gaps on their own.

Anderson goes on to say that we are called upon to improvise—that is, to put ourselves into the story and to fill in the gaps with our own experience. We must be ready to get onto the biblical stage and participate personally—along with the "company," the community of faith—in the dramatic movement of the plot, act by act. . . . It is the testimony of many generations that, when the Bible is read in the community of faith, the Holy Spirit enhances the human words of Scripture with new meaning and power. As a result, people become actors in what Amos Wilder calls "the great story and plot of all time and space and [they] are drawn into relation with God, the Great Dramatist."

The words on the pages of my little story find meaning and power in the gospel story, and it's much bigger than I can even imagine. That's where I find my little page of paper in the first place.

To understand my efforts to live out my own story in the faith heritage to which I belong, it's important to know that Churches of Christ do not have formal ordination of ministers. In many congregations, when a Christian is called to ministry, there is a set procedure of ordination, but that's not true for Churches of Christ. Some of our ministers have degrees from college or preaching school. Some of them go on to earn the master of divinity, the professional pastor's degree. But there is also openness to allowing the average male church member to preach upon occasion regardless of professional degree, such as when the full-time preacher is out of town. Or a man without ordination or degree may even preach full time in a church if that's what the church decides to do. I know of men in Churches of Christ who do not have ministry degrees but often serve professionally in the preaching role.

My husband John has a master of divinity and a PhD in philosophy and is often contacted about preaching at various congregations even though he is not serving in a church ministry role; he currently serves as the provost of Rochester College. Occasionally, it's obvious that the congregation making the request has run out of options for preachers, having no permanent or even part-time preacher available. Even when he's busy, he doesn't like to turn down a request because there's a need, and he can fill it. Sometimes he calls other male friends of ours, and together they help these churches fill their pulpits for a Sunday morning.

When John gets phone calls or e-mails about a congregation that needs a preacher, I overhear the process of several men in discussion with each other about who might fill the request to preach, and in that process I can't help but feel I could help if only it would be accepted. It's like Sarah leaning out from her tent, overhearing and hoping. John knows and appreciates my gifts and calling and has always been supportive and encouraging of my preaching. He also knows that most of the churches that call him would never consider asking a woman to preach. At one point, a Church of Christ congregation asked us to preach together, but John wasn't available on that particular Sunday even though I was. Because the opportunity was specifically tied to his presence and male leadership in the sermon, it wasn't an option for me to go without him.

I sometimes pick up *The Christian Chronicle*, a Church of Christ newspaper, and I read one listing after another in which congregations are seeking a man to preach. I know of congregations that show a video or listen to an audio recording of a sermon week after week as they wait to find a preacher. I know of congregations where boys as young as twelve are encouraged to preach on Sunday evenings as preparation for a lifetime of service to the church. In those situations, having a woman preach, even occasionally, is not considered. I understand the interpretation of Scripture that leads to the situation, but as the preacher shortage seems to grow, I find it increasingly difficult to see those opportunities pass by.

When I think of how serious our churches are about women not serving in teaching roles, I think of my friend, Ann Bryan. Ann told me of an occurrence in which she volunteered to teach Vacation Bible School at the congregation to which she and her husband, Bert, belonged at the time. She was assigned to teach the fourth to sixth grade section, and she worked in advance to make preparations for the exciting week of Bible school to come. VBS was to start on Monday morning, but on Sunday, one of the fifth grade boys decided to be baptized, a joyous occasion.

Because of that decision, however, church leaders did not think Ann, a mature woman and experienced teacher both inside and outside the church, should teach the fifth grade section. It was reasoned that because one of the boys was now a baptized believer, it would be wrong for any woman to be in a position of providing authoritative spiritual teaching to him. The night before VBS was to start, efforts were made to find a man to fill the position. When a man could not be found at that late date, Bert was asked to come into the first session on Monday morning and clarify to the fourth through sixth graders that he was turning the class over to Ann. As her husband, he was to be seen as the authority over her and by extension over the class. Ann speaks, all these years later, of how hurtful it was to her to be seen as a last-resort teacher for VBS rather than a respected and appreciated contributor. She has carried the pain of that situation with her for years now, a wound that doesn't heal easily. The suggestion that she could not be in a position of authority over a twelve-year-old, her own son's age and the age of students in her classroom at school, did not add up, and the games of semantics that were used to justify her teaching left her deflated.

Ann and Bert's story illustrates how outside the box it is to suggest that I might use my gifts and fulfill my calling in most congregations of Churches of Christ. When teaching young boys is questioned, teaching the wider congregation is not even up for discussion.

At times I have asked, "If this is a calling [and I believe it is], where did it come from? From God? From Satan? From Oprah?" God has gifted and called me and has guided me into creative situations where I can be used. God has not left my gifts latent, and perhaps precisely because I haven't been able to preach and teach in churches on many occasions, I have found that I have a gift for teaching the Bible outside the church, to those who are not regular churchgoers. I have been blessed to teach the Bible to those who are Muslim, Hindu, Bahai, shamanist, animist, agnostic, and atheist, friends who have also taught me a great deal. It's in those times of teaching that I fill the insatiable thirst related to my calling. And I find that I'm actually good at it.

I once found myself in one of those unique situations when we were living in Uganda. While we and others on our mission team love local Ugandan food, we were very pleased to have some variety when a Chinese restaurant opened in our little town of Jinja, and we quickly became friends with the Chinese owner of the restaurant, Jon. Jon had initially moved to Uganda without his wife, Yenchi, who stayed behind in China, but his plan was to bring her as soon as the business was established. After some time, Jon's restaurant was thriving, and Yenchi arrived in Uganda to join her entrepreneurial husband at their restaurant, the Ling-Ling, which means "darling little girl."

English is the official language of business in Uganda, so it was important for Yenchi to learn English as soon as possible. Jon asked around in town regarding who might teach English to Yenchi, and it was suggested that since I have an English degree, I could probably do it. Jon offered to pay me to teach her, but I declined to accept money. Jon knew that my children loved little cups of local ice cream, so instead of giving me money, every time Yenchi came for an English lesson, she brought ten cups of ice cream. Two lessons a week, ten cups of ice cream each lesson. You can do the math: We had plenty of ice cream to share with every guest who came to visit us.

So I found myself in Uganda, teaching English to a Chinese woman in exchange for ice cream. That's not a scenario I had imagined while a student at Harding University.

Although I have an English degree, I knew nothing about teaching English to a non-English speaker, and I knew nothing about Chinese languages. We communicated through charades and picture books initially, and Yenchi was immersed in English at the restaurant and a fast learner, so mostly to her credit and very little to mine, she became an English speaker and still lives in Uganda where she now contributes at their second business, a guesthouse also called the Ling-Ling. So the restaurant is the first Ling-Ling, and the guesthouse is the second Ling-Ling. When Jon and Yenchi were blessed with a beautiful daughter, she became the third Ling-Ling!

When I was studying English with Yenchi, I knew that sometimes the Bible is employed as a resource when teaching English, so I began to read parts of the Bible with her. I would select a few passages before she arrived; my main method for choosing was to find passages that had words I thought she could handle. So the passage choices were scattered. We might read a sentence in Genesis and then skip to Luke and then end up in Proverbs. As we read various passages one day, Yenchi became (understandably) frustrated with me. She closed the Bible and said, "No more little words. Tell me the big story." I realized then that she was trying to piece together all the seemingly random passages we were reading into some kind of whole, but I wasn't giving her guidance about how they all fit together.

That day I did something I had never before attempted as a Christian. I closed the Bible, and I told its story from beginning to end, explaining how it all fits together—even though there is a variety of genres, including poetry, narrative, history, and letter, and even though there is a host of authors and seemingly endless characters, and even though the Bible moves through a variety of places and cultures and languages. I found a way to explain it in very simple English in a short period of time. Yenchi became much less frustrated with reading Bible passages because she knew the context of the entire story.

That experience with Yenchi has continued to influence my teaching of Scripture. Before that experience, if I studied with someone who didn't know the Bible, I would have needed a pre-arranged guide to help me lead them through a list of passages, the goal of which was to lead the person, within one or maybe a few studies, to a decision for baptism. Those guides were linear and structured. Even though I knew the message of the Bible, I thought that in order to study with someone, I would need to have most of the Bible memorized and be able to flip about with precision to all the most important texts to prove my points. So even though I tried sharing the Bible in that way a few times, it mostly meant that I didn't engage the message of the Bible and the story of Jesus outside Christian circles at all.

The day that I realized I could tell the whole story of the Bible to Yenchi, even without preparation beforehand, I gained confidence in sharing with more people. That day when I told someone the big story that defines my own story, I knew for perhaps the first time that I was good at teaching the Bible to those who don't know it well.

I then began to find myself teaching the Bible under mango trees and in smoky cooking huts. I gained confidence in teaching the Bible. Although I had enjoyed teaching English and literature in my career before moving to Uganda, teaching the Bible connected me with what it seemed I was created to do, to my vocation, to my own calling. I began to read and study the Bible as I never had before. I was freed of formulaic reading that seeks to prove others wrong in a battle of words. I learned that the Word will take care of the words when I step into the unique calling upon my life, to teach the Bible.

I had a great amount to learn, and I had experience to gain. I was a mediocre Bible teacher, extending several years into my time as a campus minister at Rochester College. I was years behind the men my age who had been encouraged to teach the Bible authoritatively since they were very young men. I became a bit envious during that time when I noticed that men receive every encouragement when they step into the world of teaching the Bible. Parents are proud of sons who want to preach. Churches are proud of sons who want to lead worship. Professors are proud of the young men in their classrooms who excel in Greek and Hebrew. There's a sense, it seems to me, that when a community or family births a preacher or missionary, they know they are doing something right. When a young man preaches a keynote sermon at the Pepperdine Bible Lectures or the Lipscomb University Celebration gathering, pride in the young preachers is palpable on the part of those who have raised him in our schools and churches.

But, what happens when a community births a *female* preacher or missionary?

In my experience, there just isn't a category. I remember being told at times that I would make a fine preacher's wife, and then I was encouraged with the message that I was a good missionary's wife. But if I had said, "No, *I* want to be a preacher" or "I want to be a missionary," there really wasn't an understanding of what that might even mean. As a woman, the pressure *not* to make those statements is palpable.

And yet, the Holy Spirit gave me the encouragement I needed to make it through my mediocre attempts at teaching the Bible. When I first started working at Rochester College as a part-time campus minister, along with the full-time campus minister, Shannon Williams, Dr. Ken Johnson, the president of the college at the time, was affirmative and supportive as I stepped into chapel leadership. In a short time, my role became a full-time position, and when Shannon eventually left his role, I became the college's campus minister. It was during those seven years that I nervously taught Bible lessons in Rochester College's chapel, for the most part to an affirmative student body.

It wasn't, however, always affirmative. One day when I read from the Bible and spoke in chapel, a young man became angry and left the auditorium. He apparently went straight to his room and wrote an e-mails that I received upon return to my office. It read, "You said in chapel that you read your Bible, but you obviously don't read it, or you would know that it says, 'women are to be silent in the church.'"

On another occasion, I once endured a visit from an alumna of the college, who knocked on my door and started pointing at the nameplate outside my door that read, "Sara Barton, Campus Minister." She loudly insisted that I remove it, saying that no Church of Christ school could have a woman minister. I invited her into my office to sit and talk, but she refused, took my nameplate off, and threw it on the ground.

Discouraging moments are not unusual for ministers or anyone else. What was consistently unique about such events for me, however, is that they weren't based on things I said or thought or some personality quirk I have. They were based simply on the fact that I am female.

Those discouraging moments, though, were certainly few among the many affirmations I have received through the years. I have a file full of cards and notes of encouragement. A short note from my colleague Garth Pleasant is taped on the front: "Thank you for sharing your love for the Lord that your students see daily when they are in chapel."

As I matured into my gifts, God gave me a group of students who must be mentioned: Tim, Samantha, David, Lara, Sara, Lindy, Darren,

Kara, Hannah, Suzy, Chris, Kristan, Krystal, Justin, and Brandi. They were students who were already present when I arrived at RC, and they embraced me and allowed me to serve as their teacher, pastor, and mentor. Many others came along the way, but it was that first little flock that gave me the confidence to step into the calling. In many ways, they mentored me in becoming a mentor.

My husband John has been with me as a supportive partner, with his attendance at events where I teach and preach and with his prayerful participation in the discernment process of our calling together as a married couple. John was proudly the "campus minister's husband" for me as I had been the "preacher's wife" for him, and as our children became old enough to give their own affirmation and support, they spoke and wrote words of affirmation any mom loves to hear.

It was in my ministry role at Rochester College that I was asked to baptize someone into Christ, to make chaplain visits when our students were in the hospital, to accompany students to court for a variety of reasons, to provide premarital counseling, to officiate at a wedding on a couple's special day, and to officiate at a memorial service when one of my students lost her father. The pastoral roles that came along with my ministry position confirmed my call and helped me know I was writing the pages of my little story under the guidance of the big story of God. Feedback from students helped me live into the truth that young men and women need to hear about God from the masculine and feminine perspective if they are to gain a complete picture of God.

I eventually decided that my season as a campus minister was closing, and I had an opportunity to transition into a teaching role at Rochester College, where I now teach religion and English courses, primarily our introductory Bible course, Introduction to Christian Faith, which all students are required to take as a core course in our curriculum. As I teach the course, I find that I love teaching all my students, but I especially love presenting the Bible to students who don't have a strong background with the Bible. The reality in America today, according to David Gibson in an article about church literacy, is that only half of adults in the United States can name a single Gospel, and more than 60 percent do not know the first book of the Bible. Despite our bitter battles over posting the Ten Commandments, 60 percent of Americans cannot name five of them. And while Americans proudly cite the Bible as their favorite book (93 percent own one, usually the King James Version), only 5 percent are comfortable explaining what the Bible means to another person. When Christians do teach the Bible to others, the approach that is most widely accepted is a fundamentalist approach that demands unshakeable adherence to doctrinal points of view and imposes a reading experience that rejects questioning and critical thinking.

Rather than being discouraged, I see those statistics as a great opportunity to be used by God, who has called me to teach the Word. If I had been allowed to preach in my church, I don't think I would have learned what I have about reading with those outside the church. The Holy Spirit has guided me to write the pages of my story in unique ways with a wide variety of people.

I am especially indebted to my Ugandan Christian brothers and sisters for teaching me how to extend and redefine hospitality. When I read the Bible with those outside the church, I choose to consider my pastoral role with them to be hospitality, a central aspect of the missional life. When they accept my invitation to read with them, I welcome strangers into my scriptural home; and while I sometimes feel vulnerable about what they will think of my home, I know that a hospitable spirit will be central to a positive experience. While I obviously do not own Scripture in an exclusive way, I do know my way around—a beautiful benefit of being raised in Scripture-centered Churches of Christ. I am comfortable there, and I can embrace others enthusiastically as they enter the experience with me. As readers become comfortable in a hospitable environment, they share with unbelievable depth about what it means for human life to intersect with God and Scripture.

As I've become host to the story of God, rather than seeking to be a textbook expert who can show them all the answers, I realize I am emulating the tradition of Midrash, a Jewish word for "interpretation." It's about the "more" that exists as various readers bring their experiences to the text and explore it. As I host those who don't know the Bible, they don't know all the things that Christians tend to avoid. They don't know how we pick and choose what experienced Bible readers pick and choose. They don't know what's going to happen next in a story, and so there are wonderful moments of shock and surprise.

I've had a few students who sheepishly admit they are just out of jail, and they've been some of the ones who bring the story of God to life for me. I was reading with a tough Detroit guy, who had converted during his incarceration, just recently out of prison and on a new path in life. Before telling his story, I must emphasize that throughout our studies together, he had been very careful with his language around me. I was telling the story of Judah and Tamar in a group setting, and I got to the following line: "And Judah found out Tamar was pregnant, so he demanded that she should be burned to death. But, when they fetched Tamar, she brought out Judah's staff and cord and revealed, 'I am pregnant by the one who owns these. See if you recognize whose these things are'" (Gen. 38:24–25). Think about how dramatic that is when you've never heard the story before. As I shared Tamar's dramatic line, my student couldn't hold himself back and said, "Damn, she had it planned all along."

Christians don't say that kind of thing when they read the Bible! That doesn't usually happen in Sunday school. As the group leader, I chose not to address the profanity, understanding it as a response from a guy who was caught up in the story. My role of hospitality reminds me all the time that I do not control the outcome of a Bible study. The Spirit is in control. It's a delightful, joyful, colorful experience. And when I take part in it, I know that I'm filling the insatiable thirst God gave me for sharing life with others.

If Josh asked me today what I would write on my blank piece of paper, I would have a different answer than I did a few years ago. I am filling my paper as the Spirit guides, while I interact with those who are on the pages of God with me. I continue to discern my calling, and I'm thankful to those in my community who have helped in the process. It's not my calling right now to serve as an employed church minister in a Church of Christ. Preaching and teaching outside the church is where I am called to serve, at least for now.

Still, it is a shame that I and other women who are called to ministry can't come into most of our churches and talk about it. It is more than a shame; it is *wrong* that we can't come into the church and talk about it. The calling God has given me, an insatiable thirst, is to fish for people. It's a great commission. And I am to call other Christians to do the same where they live and work. My calling is more than a job, although it might involve a job. It's more than a role with a title, although it might involve a role with a title. When I teach people the message in the Bible, I consistently know in my bones that this is my calling, one that God has given me the grace and privilege to live.

part two | **puzzled**

chapter four | **prickly pears**

I grew up on a farm outside of Melbourne, Arkansas, in a little place called LaCrosse (pronounced *laaay-cross*, like you're from Arkansas; not lacrosse, like you're from England). We lived in the same house my daddy lived in when he was a boy. It was almost destroyed by a tornado in the 1930s, a tornado that killed my great-grandfather, but the house had been rebuilt and eventually passed on to my dad, along with some farmland. My dad raised cattle, farmed fescue seed, and kept a garden every summer. The kids in our family enjoyed what I considered to be a farm wonderland of adventures. We had ponies and dogs and cats and even one sheep that my sister named Homer. We had a three-wheeler back before anyone realized they were dangerous, but we escaped miraculously unscathed from our helmet-less adventures. Maybe the best part of the farm wonderland was that we had so much space in which we could safely roam. We had acres and acres of farm land. Some of the land was cultivated for my dad's fescue seed and garden, but most of it was untouched except for the cows grazing and becoming fat so they could be sold to make hamburgers and steaks. As I close my eyes and envision those fields where we adventured our childhood away, I have two main memories: prickly pears and cow patties. I'll leave the cow patties to your imagination and share a bit about the prickly pears.

My sister, Karen, and I sometimes took our Barbie dolls into the fields to play. Our Barbies swam in a real creek and camped under real stars. There was no need for our parents to buy Barbie pretend-camping-world paraphernalia for us; we had the better version in those fields. One important consideration in our Barbie field adventures was the avoidance of prickly pears, big pear-shaped cactus plants with severe needles sticking out in all directions.

On one occasion, Karen and I were planning a Barbie adventure into the fields. We packed our Barbies and their stuff into our baby-doll stroller, and as we prepared to leave, our brother, Troy, wanted to go. Troy was about three years old at the time, and maybe we were in a good mood because we said he could go, even though Barbie adventures were never quite so fun with a little brother along. It was a late fall day, so we needed to wear our coats. My mom wanted to be sure Troy didn't get too cold, so he wore his coat and hat, and she put sweat pants on top of his corduroys. We went to play on a big hill behind our house, trudging to the top. Karen pushed the baby stroller, and I held Troy's hand. We soon found the perfect place to play, about a quarter mile from our house, near the ridge of the hill where we could sometimes see coyotes howling in the moonlight on summer nights. Karen and I set up our Barbie world and entered our playtime, complete with pretend Barbie and Ken voices. Troy played around us, picking up sticks and rocks.

Suddenly, our Barbie world was interrupted by Troy's cries. We rushed to him and realized that he had fallen right onto a big prickly pear, where he was now sitting in horrible pain, perhaps stuck because his many layers of clothes made it difficult to move. Karen and I looked at each other in terror. We couldn't imagine anything worse than those needles poking through corduroys. I rescued Troy from his precarious position on the prickly pears and turned him over to survey the damage. Sure enough, prickly pear needles, large, medium, and small, were stuck into Troy's brown pants. Karen suggested that I pull Troy's pants off, and maybe the needles would come out with the pants. So off came the sweat pants. Off came the corduroys. Off came the Incredible Hulk underwear. Yet when we looked very closely, our eyes just inches from our brother's three-year-old bottom, little needles were still visible in his skin. I tried unsuccessfully to pull them out with my fingers as he continued to scream and flail his arms and legs. There was nothing else to do: Adult help was essential. I threw Troy over my shoulder like a big sack of potatoes and ran down the hill. Troy screamed the whole way, and Karen bumped along behind us with the baby stroller and Barbies. Poor Troy, he learned the hard way that fields of prickly pears must be negotiated with care.

As I shared in the last chapter, I sense God's calling to preach and teach in a church tradition where that's just not done. As frustrating as this may be, I am deeply committed to body life and working through disagreements like this as agreeably as possible. However, that doesn't mean denying my gifts, nor does it mean throwing a church temper tantrum or fracturing the body of Christ by leaving in protest. Like being in a field of prickly pears, it does mean negotiating and discerning our path with care.

Several years ago, my husband, John, and I were asked to speak about gender roles at a gathering of elders from our churches in the Detroit area. We wanted the title of those sessions to address the situation for many of the elders in our congregations as they face gender issue decisions, which, for Churches of Christ, are potentially explosive, and we settled on the title "Gender Issues in the Church: Is there a map for this minefield?" We called it a minefield to denote dramatic seriousness. Perhaps the minefield metaphor speaks to the reality that this issue may blow our churches apart. Maybe it speaks to the reality that many churches have experienced shock and dismemberment when the role of women in church ministry is discussed, as churches split and long-time members leave over the issue. Maybe the minefield metaphor works because mines, once placed in a field during a time of war, are difficult to remove even when the desire is there to remove them. I think the metaphor connotes the seriousness of the situation in our churches in that there are no safe zones. For a growing number of our churches, the matter can't be ignored, but when undertaken, it leaves little hope for a peaceful outcome.

At the Pepperdine Bible Lectures last year, several young male ministers were invited to take part in a panel discussion about women's roles in church ministries. Each shared experiences from his congregation with panel representatives from all over the nation. When the opportunity for questions from the audience came, someone asked Abilene Christian University professor Randy Harris (it's another discussion altogether about how Randy Harris got on a panel specifically labeled "young ministers"), "Randy, you travel and speak at churches all over the nation. How do you think the conversation about gender roles is going?" His answer was honest and straight, typical for Randy Harris: "It's going terribly."

As church shepherds and ministers begin to discuss gender roles in their congregations, there is great dissonance. It is going terribly in some congregations. Church of Christ congregations have faced this conversation, and women are now included fully in those congregations. But they are few. In many churches, it does not and has not and would not go well. Minefields are an apt metaphor.

Theological explosions have been common throughout Christian history. The gender controversy is not the first or last minefield we will face. In early Christianity, huge debates took place concerning the precise nature of Christ's humanity. Churches split, and bishops were exiled and died for their beliefs. Hundreds of years later, in the sixteenth century, controversies about translating the Bible into the language of common people and the sale of indulgences created a minefield of doctrinal disagreement in which women, men, and even children gave their lives as martyrs for their faith. In the seventeenth century, controversy surfaced as Galileo questioned the church's accepted model of the universe and argued that the sun, not the earth, is the center of the universe. For his efforts, Galileo was charged with heresy and put under house arrest for the remainder of his life. The controversy was a minefield. When I put the gender matter of our day in the context of some of the minefields Christianity has experienced in history (too many to list here), I realize it's certainly not the most explosive difficulty we've faced.

I've wondered whether the metaphor for this discussion should be prickly pear pastures instead of minefields. In the prickly pear pasture metaphor, the matter is not framed so violently. The journey can be experienced in a congregation as a field of prickly issues to be maneuvered through with care, to be taken seriously, but ultimately not threatening to the life of the church. In this metaphor, churches may endure some prickles for a while as they discern together, but eventually, the prickles can be removed even if it takes some time. If disagreement is not allowed to fester, the process can lead those in the unified congregation to a place of strength for having faced decisions about gender and leadership, instead of avoiding them or dividing over them.

I imagine that some readers might side with the minefield metaphor, depending on circumstances in their churches. For them, the idea of women preaching represents a journey in a destructive minefield to be avoided at almost any cost. Even taking a step in that direction may be seen as hazardous individually and corporately. Those who disagree with women's participation in church ministries do not want these prickles to be worn out with time—that's the slippery slope that many fear. They stand firmly and make a fuss in order to ensure that churches do not lose their sense of outrage when a woman preaches, prays, or even passes a collection basket. They see women's participation in church leadership as conformity with culture and disobedience to God's direct commands. For other readers, though, the matter is a prickly pear pasture, a journey to be attempted, step-by-step, with care and wisdom. At the root of our problem is whether or not we will allow the discernment process to dis-member us. Is it worth dividing the body of Christ?

I am one of a growing handful of women from Churches of Christ who have stated publicly that we are called to preach and are still mem-bers of Churches of Christ. Many other women I know who are called to preach have left our group. Those who took the professional route of divinity studies and doctoral work in order to pastor churches are leav-ing to find work, even if they were trained at Church of Christ colleges and universities. They achieved the degrees, but then there was no one to hire them, so they are now serving churches where they are needed and wanted. It's our loss. Katie Hays, a woman my age, a gifted preacher and pastor with all the right credentials from all the right schools, tried to stay, but few congregations welcomed her as a preaching minister. She gained the experience she could at congregations that hired her in associ-ate minister roles or co-teaching roles by moving all over the United States in search of Churches of Christ that were gender inclusive. She tried to stay and preach in Churches of Christ, which she loves, but eventually she left. A man in his forties with Katie's same credentials, gifts, and experi-ence would be hired at our large influential congregations, but she's not even considered. I recently heard one of those men, a thirty-one-year-old minister at a large Church of Christ, say after hearing Katie preach, "She does my job better than I do."

My calling, in partnership with John, took me on a route outside tra-ditional church walls rather than in the middle of one congregation: mis-sionary work, where my gifts were nurtured outside traditional church settings, and campus ministry work, in a Christian college environment where roles for women are not highly restricted. I received affirmation to stay around and try to find a place to minister, although it's been clear that outside the uniquely inclusive college environment where I serve, preaching in a congregation is not an option. Perhaps it is because of my route as a missionary and campus minister that I am still around. If I had maintained a course in which I sought a place in a traditional church setting, I don't know if I could still be here, either. I can see why some women have chosen other groups and been chosen by them. At one point, when I saw Katie and received her encouragement, I remember saying to her, "I need a you in my life." Katie pastors and preaches, loves and guides a congregation of the Christian Church (Disciples of Christ). She is where she should be, and I don't resent her for it. I just wish our group could have benefited from her gifts. We need a Katie in our life.

When I'm asked why I do not leave my non-denominational group and attend a church more open to leadership of women, it's a legitimate question. Why not just become Episcopalian or Methodist or join the Disciples of Christ, who have already welcomed me to preach?

For me, it's hard not to take offense at that question when it comes from one of my own, someone in my own church heritage. It's hard not to translate that question into a little shove out the door—"If you want to preach, then leave." That's like asking me (in the words of Jesus) to cut off my hand or poke out my eye. That would be particularly difficult for me since I've only one good eye. I just don't have an eye to spare. God may call John and me to leave our group someday, but for now, we strive to stay and contribute as we can in the body of Christ where we find ourselves.

My story is specific to Churches of Christ, but it certainly applies to countless churches outside my heritage, across both the evangelical and mainline church worlds. Conflict over gender and leadership roles is not unique to Churches of Christ.

I remember one Sunday that illustrates how this matter is wider than any specific denomination. On this particular day, I visited a church that identifies with the postmodern emergent movement. During worship that day, I saw some things that conservative evangelical Christians might find "different." We entered a building that was architecturally designed for a community experience. There was a coffee shop atmosphere, casual dress, young, hip crowd; as we sat "in the round," I saw an artist spray painting at a large easel throughout the entire service. A woman presented an interpretive dance as a focal point of worship. I appreciated what I experienced that day, a group of Christians creatively using a wide range of spiritual gifts that are not always acknowledged within corporate worship.

After the service, a group of students and I met with three male pastors of this congregation in their office, one big room that they all shared, with tall ceilings and bookshelves to the very top. It looked more like a page from an architectural magazine than any pastor's office I'd ever seen. I asked the ministers a question: "I noticed that other than the interpretative dance, women were not involved in your worship service today. I didn't hear a woman's voice at all. Does that reflect common practice here?" One of the ministers shared that although they can do pretty much anything to be "outside the box" when it comes to worship—art, dance, secular music—the one area where they had not been able to change practice without inciting conflict concerned the gender role issue. He said that some, perhaps many, members would leave if a woman took part in public leadership and that parameters about gender inclusion were central to the founding leaders of their church.

I was stunned. I had thought members could do almost *anything* at a church like that (admittedly, churches in the emergent conversation are all different, "autonomous" like my own church, so all emergent churches can't be lumped together). I wondered how this particular church came to a theological place in which a woman could dance for the church in her jeans and T-shirt on Sunday morning, but not preach.

I tell that story because even though *my* story occurs in one specific group, it is not unique to Churches of Christ. Women in churches all across the denominational spectrum are marginalized. It's because of women across all denominational lines that I am willing to discuss my journey publicly, whether it's through a minefield or a prickly pear pasture. When I tell my story, women of all ages and from all kinds of backgrounds come out of the woodwork to tell me that they want to say what I'm saying, but because of their families or their churches or their personalities, they just can't make their thoughts known. Many folks in Churches of Christ all over the country, in places from Searcy, Arkansas, to Houston, Texas, to Malibu, California, to Flint, Michigan, might be surprised what their daughters, women of all ages, have made known to me in e-mails, letters, and phone calls: that they secretly hope for change but do not speak up because they will offend their own churches, their own parents, and sometimes their own children. Families have secrets, and secrets can fester, so I'm speaking up for some sisters who can't do so just yet.

But it's only partially because of my sisters. Holistically, it's because of my brothers, too. Just as often, men tell me that they want the matter acknowledged and changed. Just as often, they tell me that they want to hear women teach and that they want to lead alongside their sisters in Christ. Some men want to take this journey with the women they know and love. When I once spoke publicly about women serving in leadership roles, a man sat on the back row in the audience with tears running down his cheeks while I was speaking. Later, he told me that his mother, who is deceased, had grown up desiring to be a Methodist pastor. She had met and married his father, a member of Churches of Christ, and they had spent their lives in our churches. This man said that he was just beginning to realize what his mother had sacrificed all those years.

It's because of women and men—because of a whole body of Christ full of sisters and brothers—that I seek to navigate these minefields and prickly pear pastures.

Just as I write from the perspective of a specific church group, I also write from a specific upbringing. My faith journey represents a specific human story, but I hope that in telling it, I will encourage others to contemplate their own faith journeys and how God is calling them in unique ways. That's how testimony works. This is my testimony.

I was baptized as a teenager at a memorable revival after a good, fire-and-brimstone sermon delivered by a well-known fire-and-brimstone kind of preacher, Jimmy Allen. I love my church and feel that this heritage is my family. Everything good in my life has come from Jesus Christ, and this fellowship of believers has been used powerfully to help me know and follow him. It was on that night, at that revival, in a special congregation, that I made a decision that has changed every decision and every moment of the rest of my life.

I attended Harding University, a Church of Christ institution in Searcy, Arkansas, not far from the town where I grew up. That's where I met my husband John and made significant lifelong friendships and was taught and mentored by godly people. After graduation, John and I lived in Memphis, Tennessee, where I taught high school English and speech while John went to graduate school to earn his master of divinity degree. During that time, he preached at a small congregation outside of Memphis, the New Hope Church of Christ, a group that rented the local Jewish synagogue for weekly Sunday services and where the older members taught us what it means to be loved and nurtured by a small church of grace-filled believers who truly have new hope.

After those years, we moved to Uganda with a mission team comprised of our close friends from college to plant more churches. John and I lived there for eight years, and our team was part of initiating a movement that now numbers over seventy churches in the Busoga region of Uganda. Now, all these years later, those churches are ministering to us as we continue to minister to them. I cannot imagine my life without the influence of Ugandan Christians.

Since leaving Uganda, I have worked as both a professor and campus minister at Rochester College in Michigan, a college founded over fifty years ago by members of Churches of Christ. In short, I've lived my life and ministered in one faith heritage. I love this group of believers. I am thankful for them. I am proud to be one of them. They nurtured me as a child, educated me as a college student, introduced me to my husband, supported our mission work efforts, and provided me with friends too numerous to mention. Now this group is doing the same for our children. I am indebted to my faith heritage, indebted in the most positive sense.

In churches from Arkansas to Tennessee to Uganda to Michigan, this issue of gender roles has been with me all my life. There was something in me from a very young age that wanted to lead and organize and plan and teach—and to do that as part of church. As a little girl, I had an interest in sermons, and I took notes on sermons even before I turned ten years old. I had opinions as a preteen about what our preacher said and how he illustrated his lessons. The sermon I remember most clearly and specifically from my years of growing up was about the body of Christ, preached by our minister, Tom Brister. Tom is a gentle, kind preacher, and in that particular sermon, he opened my mind to how all the members of the body of Christ function together, take care of one another, and enable one another to serve God uniquely together. He prompted me to think about my own place in the body of Christ, and his sermons affected me, as I believe sermons are designed to do. I went home, and I contemplated and prayed about my role within my church body. I can remember, for example, practicing public prayers in my mind and thinking about how I would say a prayer aloud if ever I did. Looking back, I wonder why I did that. I had no models for this; Joyce Meyer wasn't on TV back then. The musings seemed to come from nowhere, and I was not sure what to do with them.

I eventually found reason for more confusion mixed with some encouragement as our congregation began to participate in the church leadership program for young people that I mentioned earlier. I was encouraged to write and present lessons from the Bible, pray, read Scripture, and memorize God's Word. While it was clear that these acts of leadership were confined to gatherings of women only, I found that this program helped me connect with the passion I had for being used by God. I felt alive and useful.

As a college student, I took a career assessment designed to help discover one's ideal job, and the top result was "expository preacher." I remember holding the paper that gave me this strange outcome, and all I knew to do was laugh. I showed it to one friend, Brent, and I remember he was encouraging and said that I would be really good at that. I wondered what was wrong with Brent.

I considered majoring in Bible in college, but I was much too practical for that. There was one female student in the Bible Department when I was at Harding in the late 1980s. Christy was an anomaly to me. I heard people wonder about what she would do to support herself if she didn't get married. We knew there certainly would not be a job for her anywhere that we could imagine. I majored in English with a minor in Bible. I wanted to do what I saw Christy doing, but I was afraid. And I sure didn't know what to do with the results of my career assessment. I made a joke of it because I couldn't imagine what else to do.

My desire to teach and preach began to bring about significant dissonance when I found myself working with churches in Uganda. While there, I presented Bible studies for women. I would send out letters of invitation to new churches and invite women to study the Bible with me in certain villages. Then I would drive our big four-wheel-drive vehicle over the bumpy roads and arrive, ready for my little ladies' events, only to find that more often than not, women showed up, but so did men, men who were church leaders themselves. As they arrived, they came with Bibles in hand, eager to learn. I thought, "Didn't they read my invitations? *This is a women's event.* We never had this problem at our ladies' events in Arkansas."

Early on, I told the men to leave. I was uncomfortable talking in front of them. I was worried about what our supporting churches would say if I taught men. I wanted in every fiber of my being to do what was right in the eyes of my church, and the situation in which I found myself was outside our missionary training.

But there I was with people who wanted to study the Bible, and our missionary men didn't have time to go to every preaching point and fulfill every teaching need. So somewhere along the way, I stopped telling the men to leave. I taught in these informal settings under the shade of trees as goats wandered in and out of our midst, and we all learned about God and Scripture from each other.

Another challenge arose when one of the Ugandan church leaders saw a high school speech textbook on the bookshelf in our house and asked me about it. When I told him that American schools offer speech classes and that I had taught those classes before coming to Uganda, he asked me to teach a speech class to men who wanted to learn more about public speaking—so they could gain some training for preaching in their churches. I said yes to this request and soon found myself teaching a group of men to make speeches *about* God, *about* the Bible. I was teaching men to preach. I remember asking myself at one moment on the first day of that class, "How have I gotten myself into this predicament?" At a church service soon after that class, one of the men, a leader in the church, spontaneously called upon me to say the closing prayer. I said the prayer, but later one of the missionary men (who kindly asked my thoughts first) spoke to the church leader and told him he shouldn't call upon women to pray publicly because it wasn't part of the practice of Churches of Christ.

It was at the time of that little preaching class in Uganda that I decided I had to explore this issue about what God desires regarding women's leadership in churches. What a journey it has been. It has been challenging and hard and rewarding and interesting and frustrating and freeing and validating and controversial. I have been blessed on this journey as it has brought me closer to God and made me more complete in my understanding of who I am as a human made in God's image. I have been challenged to explore how I am to relate to all the members of Christ's church, of the same body of Christ that I am, whether we agree on this issue or not, whether we journey through minefields or a pasture of prickly pears.

This journey has led me down paths that I cannot avoid.

I cannot retreat to teachings and practices I was given as a young girl and solve this matter. They don't fully address many aspects of the subject, and there is too much at stake. My conviction is that churches have been wrong in denying women the blessing of using their gifts in the body of Christ, whatever their gifts may be: teaching Sunday school, or contributing accounting skills to the budget process, or caring for widows in the church, or leading the church as a preacher or an elder.

My ideas are not easy for me to explain to many people I respect. Saying I want to preach and teach is a real conversation stopper, and it seems easier at times just to be silent.

Unity is tremendously important to me. Little on earth is better than Christian unity. I believe unity is at the core of who God is. We see in the Genesis account of creation that God made us for community and oneness in diversity, modeled by the Father, the Son, and the Spirit. Something inherent in our humanity beckons us to community. Unfortunately, because creation is fractured, we aren't very good at the very community for which we hunger and thirst. In his book *Simply Christian*, N. T. Wright makes clear that humans were created for unity in relationships. He points out that we long for it deep in our bones. When I think of the discussion of gender roles in churches, I have to wonder what to do about unity. This controversial topic could tear our churches apart, like explosions in a minefield.

One of the biblical texts closest to my heart is Philippians chapter two, "[I]n humility, value others above yourselves, not looking to your own interests but each of you to the interests of others. In your relationships with one another, have the same attitude of mind Christ Jesus had" (vv. 3b–5). How do I embody Christlike humility in relation to the controversy regarding gender roles? As I try to look to the interests of others, I see those I love.

I see Lindy, a graduate of Rochester College, one of the finest Christian leaders we've ever had on our campus. After graduation, Lindy worked as a planter of house churches in the Bronx, partially supported by my home congregation. Once, when Lindy was presenting a report of her work during the Sunday morning service, other friends of mine were also visiting, people I respect greatly. They came from a church where a woman would not be allowed to give a report like Lindy was giving, and they could not conscientiously be in the room when Lindy was speaking. They quietly left the auditorium when Lindy started toward the front, before she even said a word. How do I look to the interests of my three friends whom I love?

I also see Judy. Judy feels scared when we discuss the gender question, because while others do not see it as a "salvation issue," she believes it is. She has always been taught that it is an issue that affects eternal salvation, and she fears for the eternal souls of herself and her children and grandchildren if the church gets this issue wrong. Palpable fear motivates Judy, and she thinks if we open leadership roles to women, we might all spend eternity in hell.

Then I see Lew, an elder, who is caught between the opinions of his wife and his parents and his children, whose convictions vary radically on the gender debate. As an elder, a husband, a father, and a son, he can't make anyone happy in the end because the church is seen as moving either too fast or too slow, no matter what decision he and the other elders make on the matter.

I look to the interests of others, and I see Anita. She has given forty years of her life to teaching Sunday school, driving widows to church, and making her best apple cake for church potlucks. She takes some of my language about women's roles as if I am saying that her contributions have not been important.

I see Chris, a worship minister at a Church of Christ who personally wants women to participate in leading worship, but he must balance the opinions of the elders and the staff and the congregation. He's often stuck in the middle of controversy instead of in the middle of worship, which is where he longs to be.

There's Katy, a young, energetic, opinionated, Christian woman who is majoring in Biblical Studies. She is thoroughly satisfied with the explanation that gender roles are related to cultural context, and she wonders, "What is the big deal?" She thinks it's just weird that our services are dominated by men in the same American society of the twenty-first century.

There's James, who feels that his own marriage will no longer make sense if gender roles are redefined. He's lived for twenty-four years as the head of his household, and when his wife wants to discuss changing their relationship both at home and in church, he feels confused about his life: Were the past twenty-four years a mistake?

And I see Ida, a Ugandan woman who leads churches in Busoga. She is the first person to show up at a funeral and the first person to cook for large gatherings. She is a gifted song leader, and she reads well, a gift for the church in Uganda. Ida is a teacher at heart, and yet she tells me that, in her words, "she suffers" because after years of using her gifts freely, she was told by a short-term American visitor to Uganda that it's sinful for her to speak in a public gathering of Christians.

I see Kenneth, who just gets mad (veins popping out kind of mad) when I bring it up.

And I see Missy, a mother who spends her days homeschooling her children, who wants to participate in public worship roles and who has so much to teach the rest of us about gentleness and life lived in the Holy Spirit.

I look to the interests of others, and I see my daughter.

Her name is Brynn. She's an amazing young woman. Sixteen years old now.

In a church setting several years ago, a man came up to our family and asked if some of us could help distribute flyers during the service, and the first person to volunteer was my Brynn. Brynn is not shy or hesitant when help is needed. She wants to help in positive ways at church. Yet the man looked at us uncomfortably and said, "I was thinking this is the kind of job that is just for the guys." Her eager face turned confused and deflated.

Brynn and her brother, Nate, often serve the congregation by passing communion trays during the service we attend at our congregation. As gender roles have been addressed, it has been decided by our elders, that in our different services, we will approach the matter in different ways. In one service of the congregation, for example, women did not initially pass communion trays, but they did in the service we regularly attended. Once when we attended the service in which women did not participate, Brynn said to me, "Mom, I feel bad when I come to this service because Nate is allowed to pass trays, and I am not."

I look to the interests of Brynn, and I have to wonder if she is already being conditioned to think her brother Nate is needed by God and needed at church more than she is. I look to the interests of Nate, and I see that he has opinions about these matters, opinions that include a desire for full participation of both genders.

Talking to all these different people and yearning for unity deep in my bones, wanting our relationships to be about Jesus Christ and not defined by controversy, sometimes it seems we're from different planets and speaking different languages. I wonder how unity in Christ can survive among us. I wonder if the explosive metaphor is the right one—a minefield that will dismember us all.

Perhaps we should consider what it was like for early Christians as they embarked on a journey for unity in diversity. What was it like when they looked around in their gatherings and considered others above themselves? I look back in time, and I picture a bearded, pious, Jewish man who had recently found his Messiah, Jesus of Nazareth. I wonder what it was like for him to attend worship services with a Gentile. He was taught from the time he was a little boy that Gentiles are unclean and disobedient to God—and now he is called to unity, to oneness with them? He is called to redefine everything that ever made sense to him. How did he traverse the minefield in front of him? How did he put unity above himself and his long-held beliefs and comfort?

I think about women in the early church. I picture two women in conversation, one of them wearing a head covering while in public, who has never shown her hair to any man besides her husband because she considers it immodest to do so. She is called to unity with a sister, a sophisticated Corinthian woman who has her hair done in a showy fashion, and I wonder—what did they talk about? How did they worship together? What major life beliefs were they called to redefine through the power of the Holy Spirit? What was it like for them to seek unity together on prickly issues?

I think about Philemon and wonder what it was like when he was with Onesimus, after he got a letter from Paul urging him to accept this slave, *this man he owned*, as a brother in Christ. I wonder about the relationship of slaves and masters in churches. I imagine that it was more than awkward and that unity must have been a challenge. I imagine that explosions took place over this issue of humanity that life in Jesus Christ calls us to address.

In the Philippian church, Paul challenged two women quite directly about unity. I wonder what it was like for Eudia and Syntyche as they listened to the reading of Paul's letter, probably at their church, and there in front of everyone they were very specifically and publicly called to unity. We don't know what their problem was, but it was so significant that Paul directly called them to strive for the same attitude of mind Christ Jesus had. Their situation must have been emotional. It must have involved weighty matters to warrant the attention of that letter. It must have been a minefield in their lives.

The early church faced explosive issues of unity like the one we now face with gender roles.

Emotional topics are not new.

Prickly topics are not new.

Pursuit of unity is not new.

But nowhere in Scripture do I see that Christians are released from Paul's encouragement in Philippians 2: "[I]n humility value others above yourselves, not looking to your own interests but each of you to the interests of the others" (vv. 3b–4).

I've struggled to understand what that means. I've just comprehended the very tip of the iceberg, the very shadow of the reality. What I know so far is that it means doing what Jesus did:

> In your relationships with one another, have the same attitude of mind Christ Jesus had: Who, being in very nature God, did not consider equality with God something to be

used to his own advantage; rather, he made himself nothing by taking the very nature of a servant, being made in human likeness. And being found in appearance as a human being, he humbled himself by becoming obedient to death—even death on a cross! Therefore God exalted him to the highest place and gave him the name that is above every name, that at the name of Jesus every knee should bow, in heaven and on earth and under the earth, and every tongue acknowledge that Jesus Christ is Lord, to the glory of the Father. (Phil. 2:5–11 TNIV)

You can look at all the classic scriptures on the gender topic, and I encourage you to do so. I've looked in depth at Genesis 2, Galatians 3, 1 Timothy 2, Ephesians 5, 1 Corinthians 11, 1 Corinthians 14. I have studied these and other texts. I have prayed. I have sought guidance from wise people. And I have formulated opinions. I have to admit that at times I have struggled against pride. I want everyone to read these scriptures the way I read them and come to the conclusions that I do.

That's not humility.

I have been angry and have spoken disrespectfully of very good people. I have lost hope and resentfully considered leaving my church.

That's not humility.

That's not unity.

My appeal to Paul's words in Philippians chapter two may sound naïve as churches face explosive decisions about gender and leadership. These words may not provide the textual proof that some would like to have to "solve" it. It's my opinion that we cannot settle this by appealing to isolated texts. Historically, isolated texts have been used to argue both sides of the gender debate, and I think it's pointless to pursue that path. That pursuit has not brought unity but division. That's where my understanding of Scripture differs from some others. I am determined to look not at isolated texts within Scripture but at broad theological themes and redemptive movements informed by an understanding of the gospel, which then becomes the basis for reading those texts, not in isolation but in context. As I wander through those prickly theological texts, my challenge, my command, my example, my every intention is to have the same mindset Christ Jesus had, one that humbly gives up power and serves unselfishly. As I see it broadly, few doctrinal issues should dismember us. The statement, "Jesus is Lord," for example, is central for Christians, to the point of death as illustrated in the life of the early church. As for the rest, we are to seek communal discernment in our day and time and in our relationships with one another on a journey guided by the same attitude of mind Christ Jesus had.

If these words about relationships were important to ancient Christians as Paul encouraged them to live lives worthy of the gospel, then they are important for you and me as we face the journey of how we will live lives worthy of the gospel.

It's when I put the journey in the context of the example of Jesus Christ that I see the journey as a prickly pear pasture rather than a minefield. Although we may not be in full agreement, if we all pursue the same attitude that Christ Jesus had, then we will be able to take the careful journey together. Getting poked by a prickly pear when you're all alone would not be a good experience, but if we are with brothers and sisters who pick us up when we fall down and take care of our wounds, then the prickles don't hurt quite so badly or for quite so long. Whatever decisions a church makes regarding questions of gender roles, some people will get poked. Some people will get hurt. But if, in our relationships with one another, we have the same attitude Christ Jesus had, regardless of our church backgrounds, we need not experience dismemberment and irreversible pain.

One point is clear: If wounds are left to fester, they can kill just like an explosion can kill. Whether it's a minefield or a prickly pear pasture, we must face the gender discussion with Spirit-led prayer and discernment in a loving, trusting, Christ-centered community.

I made the mistake one day of Googling *women preachers*. Here are some samplings of what I found in some articles and blogs that exhibit attitudes that are not Christ-centered:

"Women preachers are repulsive."

"If the Bible is clear on the fact that women must be silent in the church, then how can some women make the claim that 'they have been called to preach?' Very simple, with ignorance of and disdain for Scripture, even the sodomite can be 'called' to preach."

"If women claim they have been called to preach, we can know instantly that they are liars or deceived."

"When a woman rebels against God by usurping authority over men, a host of other sins follow."

"Women preachers are all false prophets."

"Women have cited Balaam's donkey as an argument that they should be able to preach. Their argument puts them even lower than an ass."

It's my hope that instead of exhibiting the attitude seen on my Google search, we'll model for our children and the world how believers may walk through these difficult issues with a heart of love and respect for those with whom we differ.

One Easter Sunday at my congregation a few years ago I received just that kind of respect from a friend. I was struggling so severely with this issue that I could not worship on this important day—Easter Sunday! I wanted to worship, but I felt like an outsider, like I didn't belong there, as if I were speaking a language that no one else understood because I was so "liberal" when it came to discussions about women's roles in church ministries. I thought that if I told anyone what my opinions were on the topic, I would not be accepted in that body of Christ. I struggled through worship, and I struggled to participate in communion with my church body.

When it was announced that elders were standing at the back, ready to pray with anyone who had concerns, I knew that I had to ask for prayers.

As I went to the back, I have to admit that I hoped to see one of the elders who might come close to agreeing with me and understanding me, someone I perceived to be "progressive" on the issue. But instead, I found Jerry Felzien, whom I respect and appreciate but who tends to be more traditional than I am. I almost didn't tell him my concerns. But I was desperate, and Jerry was who God gave me, so I told Jerry how I felt. He took me into our quiet prayer room, listened to me intently, and prayed that I would feel accepted by my church family. Notably, he did not try to correct my thinking on the subject. Even though he didn't agree with me doctrinally, he exhibited the same attitude of mind of Christ Jesus himself on that day, and he has continued to live out that theme of love for the years that have followed. On that day, through Jerry's kindness, I found a companion with whom to walk in pastures of prickly pears. Sometimes I feel like the little child, crying because I've sat squarely on a prickly issue. Sometimes I realize that maybe I've knocked someone down as they've traversed the field. But in this field of faith, I have continued to pray that God will help me to experience others through the mind of Jesus, the perfecter of faith.

chapter five | **putting the pieces together**

I love to walk in the woods, especially in autumn. Near my house, the fall leaves create a golden canopy where I walk and talk with Jesus, singing old hymns. Not long ago I was walking under that golden canopy, and it occurred to me to contemplate what I might say to Jesus if he were physically there with me. My time during that walk had been spent simply being with him, not pondering one specific topic of conversation. I thought, if I really believe he's present, why don't I just walk up to him in these woods and ask him if what women do—or do not do—in church ministry is at the center of the gospel? I want to know if the issue is one of the *big issues*. I wish I could meet him in the woods physically for just a moment, see his face, and hear his voice. There is a difference in being present spiritually and being present physically. Both are realities, but in God's mysterious wisdom, he invites us into a spiritual reality instead of giving us a physical one. I hope that if I were to meet Jesus physically in those woods, I would be so overcome with his presence that I would fall to my knees in worship. I would probably embarrass myself if I tried to enter a theological discussion.

All the same, I am a curious soul, and if I could ask just one question of a physically present Jesus, what would it be? Would I say, "Jesus, what do you think about women preachers?" But that's not what it all really comes down to, is it? Maybe if I had only one question, I would try to squish a variety of our disputed topics into that one opportunity. How could I include all of it—miraculous healing, tongue-speaking, communion observance, best preaching practices, house church versus institutional church, big church versus small church, loud bands versus simple singing, leadership roles, gender roles. Hmmm, could I fit it all into one question if I really tried?

Perhaps I could ask, "What's the greatest rule?" Or "What's the greatest doctrinal issue?" Or—I've got it—"What's the greatest commandment?"

Oh wait, somebody already did that.

In Matthew 22, Jesus was asked what's ultimately at the center. That's what those old Pharisees were up to when one of them inquired, "What is the greatest commandment?" Perhaps they had all been sitting around discussing how they could fit all their issues into one big question opportunity. Maybe they had been trying to figure out how to get the answer that would apply to their myriad of questions and issues. They likely had been trying to catch Jesus in a doctrinal riddle of sorts, so some legalist came up with the question, "What is the greatest commandment?"

Jesus answered their trick question with this statement: "Love the Lord your God with all your heart, with all your soul, and with all your mind . . . and love your neighbor as yourself" (Matt. 22:37, 39b). He said that *all* the law and prophets hang on these two commandments. I wonder if I would stand there, a bit deflated, a bit puzzled perhaps, with those old Pharisees thinking, "Well, *that's* an evasive answer." All of the doctrines? All of the worship wars? All of the issues that cause our comfort or discomfort in worship? All of the answers to our questions? It would be a bit disappointing, an uncomfortable moment for sure, if

I spent my one Jesus question, and I didn't even get a definitive answer to *my* heart's issue.

It's uncomfortable that these words are Jesus' definition of the greatest commandments when we're trying to figure out religious doctrines and worship practices. When I seek the heart of the matter in the midst of diverse interpretations of the texts around the controversy of women in church ministries, I have to remind myself that they all hang on two commands about love. If you are feeling a bit unsatisfied, uncomfortable, perhaps frustrated with the love direction of this doctrinal conversation, then you're in the same place I am, and you're in the same place as the original askers of the question—"What is the greatest commandment?" Jesus is, uncomfortably, about love. Being his disciple is about love, and living out the love answers Jesus gives for our life questions is a continual challenge. We will never experience a feeling of utter conclusion until *he* returns to conclude all of life and its questions. Jesus is the love answer to our questions, but we have to let him be the mysterious answer. That's faith.

I have spent my life trying to piece together the answers to life's myriad questions, ultimately concerning my calling as a Christian. That's the idea for all of us—inhabiting this mysterious life the best we can with eyes of faith focused on Jesus, regardless of what difficult questions may arise. We are called to traverse life with our eyes on our Lord, not simply in light of what we've always been taught.

I grew up in the 1970s and '80s, when changing attitudes toward gender were explored on levels beyond the curious fashion styles (picture masculine shoulder pads for women) of that time. Times were changing, and many were not sure what to do or say concerning changing gender roles; therefore, except for outspoken feminists, many conflict-avoiding Americans did not speak aloud of the changing roles. For all of us, it's simply more comfortable to keep difficult transitions quiet and avoid discord than to speak of them out loud. In my life, cultural change, especially as it relates to gender roles, was not addressed openly for a variety of reasons. This unspoken nature of gender roles left my generation and me with clues to an enigmatic puzzle. Gender roles were changing around me, but there was no picture on the puzzle box to illustrate how my life was supposed to fit in with the lives of my role models. On the one hand, I had role models like my grandmothers and great-grandmothers, who lived in traditional roles while also embodying the kind of strength that sustained them through the Great Depression and sending husbands and sons to war. On the other hand, women like Samantha Stevens, Mary Tyler Moore, Murphy Brown, and three very sexy angels entered my living room and challenged traditional definitions of what it means to be a strong woman.

The drastic shift in gender roles that took place around the time of my birth, in the 1960s, cannot be underestimated. I was born into a situation in which human hierarchy concerning gender was being questioned unlike any other time before (civil rights for African Americans was also central to the tumult of that time period, an important element of American history, but not the tumult I am discussing here, concerning gender specifically).

In the Busoga region of Uganda, on the other hand, hierarchy still is not questioned as it has been in the Western world. Hierarchy is clear. It is taught. It is physically embodied as early as possible. Little girls are taught to kneel to men as early as they can stand, so they cannot even remember when they were first taught this distinction between genders. There is no question that men call the shots, head the clans, lead the families, and make the decisions. This is perhaps similar to what women in America experienced just a few generations ago. For the most part, women did not kneel physically, but our great-grandmothers had their physically embodied definitions of what it meant to be the weaker sex. Education level, style of clothing, physical and emotional demeanor, hairstyle, birth control methods, travel opportunities . . . we could keep going. All of these former gender differences intertwine with our definitions of hierarchy, and they have specifically defined cultural shifts in American life as I've known it since my birth in 1968.

As I sorted out my place in the world, I especially loved the church and wanted to sort out my gender role questions in that arena of thought. Some of my first memories are of playing church. My brother Dave played church as the preacher. He sweated. He paced. He wiped his brow. He preached "old style." And, the family cheered him on. It was an act he performed, one of those fun family games. Several years later, my younger brother Troy played church as the song leader. He called out the number in the hymnal so that everyone could turn to the proper page in the pretend songbook, and then he flailed his arm up and down, back and forth, while everyone sang along with him. (Unrelated personal indulgence: When we got tired of Troy's song leader act, we would switch gears and say, "Get mad, Troy," and he would transform from a song leader to being the Incredible Hulk. Troy would then flex his muscles and hold his breath until his face turned red, and we all pretended he was turning green. The song leader and the Hulk were Troy's best roles, so I have to mention them both.)

In my earliest memories, I noted that the only part for a girl in our little church game was pew sitter. For a girl, it was a lot more fun to play a secular game, *Charlie's Angels*, where there was only one main part for a boy (and not a very fun part).

But as I began to find myself drawn to church work, I remember practicing prayers in my mind—prayers I imagined saying at the podium at church. Kids all have their daydreams. Playing in the NBA. Being crowned Miss America. A job as a dinosaur-excavating paleontologist. Why haven't I met any paleontologists as an adult, since so many little boys I knew said they wanted to be one? For some reason, my childhood daydreams were of church leadership, which has turned out to be as likely as excavating dinosaurs.

One of my play activities was reading a book of the Bible and writing an outline for how I would teach that book. When I was about twelve, I had a notebook I divided into sections for books of the Bible, from Genesis to Revelation; I would clip *Reader's Digest* articles that I thought would help me illustrate lessons from specific scriptures as I organized my little lesson notebook. From that notebook, I created baseball-themed Bible curriculum for teaching Sunday school kids at church. As a teenager, I wrote a series of sermons from the book of Acts. I remember my opening illustration and the introduction to my lesson that I memorized: "In 1848, gold was discovered in Sacramento, California. The news of the gold discovery spread like wildfire. In the book of Acts, Christianity spread like wildfire." As may be surmised, I was a geeky girl.

After I recently spoke at a conference in Nashville, Tennessee, about my childhood call to church life, a man I did not know said to me afterwards, "I have never supported the idea of women preaching. I did not think that God would call a woman to preach, but as I heard you describe your childhood interest in church and your innate passion for Scripture, I realized that your story paralleled mine. I cannot deny that, from my experience, this is how God called me to ministry." Unlike this preacher, however, who heard the call in his youth and found his place in the church, as I was drawn to church leadership, I found I had pieces to a puzzle but no guidance for how to put the puzzle together and no support from a community to help me recognize the call.

The gender hierarchy in many of our church services is physically embodied, based on where we sit, where we stand, the voices that are heard, the official name tags, and the prominence of male names in the church bulletin.

Think for a moment what it's like for a little girl growing up in that culture, which perhaps metaphorically gives her puzzle pieces with no box and no picture. That little girl tries to define the hierarchy in church and society from mixed-up messages. In kindergarten, she is told that every little boy and girl can be whatever he or she wants to be. On *Sesame Street* (which was born one year after I was), she sees male and female doctors, male and female construction workers. In politics, she sees Margaret Thatcher as the prime minister of a powerful country. She sees Hillary Clinton as the first lady of her state, later of the United States, as a presidential candidate, and as Secretary of State. Let's just say I have heard Hillary Clinton called every kind of name you can think of—with the *f*-word (feminist) spoken as a curse word. I was privileged to meet Hillary Clinton on several occasions when I was a teenager and more than once as an adult. Hillary Clinton, even though some may not appreciate the fact, has served as a role model to my generation for our entire lives. She's a piece of my puzzle that the church might try to keep out of the puzzle box, but little and big girls like me, whether blue or red politically or right or left theologically, still have to figure out where to put that puzzle piece of experience. For a generation now, the church has left our little girls with some confusing life pieces to assemble with little or no overt instruction. And then the little girls, now big girls, find that the church is angry that they have put puzzles together with a picture the church doesn't want.

Our little girls today, even more than I did perhaps, are growing up in a culture that sends mixed messages. Logically, churches need to either become more explicit in definitions of hierarchy or forge consistency in their practices. They can say out loud that men are the only leaders at church and in the home and then explain why that is so with teaching that goes beyond proof texting. If they do, I strongly believe they must confront the real consequences for women and men alike of taking that position. In what I'm convinced is a holier alternative, we can all rethink and prevent the confusion we are creating for our children.

A friend recently shared a statement her daughter made that would be funny if it weren't so sad. In their church, apparently little girls and boys individually may quote scriptures they've memorized in front of the congregation. They also sometimes sing in front of the congregation. They participate in dramatic readings and are often featured on videos talking about stories from the Bible. In all these activities, the little girls and boys participate in the same ways: No distinction is made between how boys and girls participate. At some point along the way, however, when they are teenagers, the situation changes, and young women are no longer asked to participate individually in speaking before the congregation, while young men are still included. This all goes unsaid; the rules are not addressed publicly. The situation becomes a disconnected puzzle piece. My friend's daughter said:

"I figured it out, Mom."

"What?" Mom said back.

"I figured out girls in church."

"What did you figure out about girls in church?" asked Mom.

"Girls can do stuff in church till they get breasts."

If we think our little girls are not putting together a confusing puzzle of gender roles in church and society, we need to think again. In our society today, there's no way around it; our little girls gain a message that it's their developing bodies that define them and give their lives meaning. They are holding pieces of a puzzle, and this family conversation shows how one little girl brought the two puzzle pieces together. An inherent part of humanity is for members of both genders to watch what goes on around them (and in their own bodies) and to figure out their place in it all. It's also an inherent part of being a Christian for men and women, boys and girls to figure out God's calling in their lives, but the church must be explicit about what that means for girls and women in their own culture and society. Otherwise, our children will turn primarily to society for meaning rather than to the church, an issue I will discuss further in a later chapter.

For me, the questions that arose for years, the questions that haunted me, prayer after prayer and study after study, boiled down to questions related to a handful of scriptures and how I had been taught to interpret them. I found, as I contemplated the puzzle before me, that I was first provided a piece of the puzzle labeled 1 Corinthians 14:34–35, which includes the passage, "Women should remain silent in the churches. They are not allowed to speak but must be in submission as the law says. If they want to inquire about something, they should ask their own husbands at home; for it is disgraceful for a woman to speak in the church."

It was easy to attach other jigsaw pieces from the box to this one. The little crevices and corners interlocked smoothly when it came to a puzzle piece like the one found in 1 Timothy 2:11–12: "A woman should learn in quietness and full submission. I do not permit a woman to teach or to assume authority over a man; she must be silent." That piece configured with another puzzle piece in Ephesians 5:22–23: "Wives, submit to your husbands as to the Lord. For the husband is the head of the wife as Christ is the head of the church, his body, of which he is the Savior." That piece, in turn, helped me link to another section from Genesis 3:16: "To the woman he said, 'I will greatly increase your pains in childbearing; with painful labor you will give birth to children. Your desire will be for your husband, and he will rule over you.'" The tab on that piece found its place with another bit of the puzzle from 1 Peter 3:1a: "Wives, in the same way be submissive to your husbands."

As I contemplated my place in the life of God, I began to see that the center of the puzzle (at least it was the center of the puzzle from everything I was taught) was coming together with some clarity. As I continued to ponder, with a deep interest in Scripture and in the life of the church, I would pick up an odd piece of the puzzle like this one found in Acts 2:17–18: "In the last days, God says, I will pour out my Spirit on all people. Your sons and daughters will prophesy, your young men will see visions, your old men will dream dreams. Even on my servants, both men and women, I will pour out my Spirit in those days, and they will prophesy."

I would hold that strange-looking, amoeba-like piece of the puzzle in my fingers. I would survey its odd contours with my eyes. I would imagine how it might fit with the puzzle I had begun. I would occasionally attempt to jam one of its strange little edges into a tab in my developing life puzzle. The fit, however, was awkward, and my puzzle wouldn't comply with my attempts.

As I continued to assemble the puzzle, I began to notice more and more pieces with all their little innies and outies that didn't fit with my observation of the center of the puzzle. A puzzle enthusiast knows that putting a puzzle together may sometimes mean joining edge pieces or creating more than one large section before comprehending how all the parts make a whole. What one once considered the center might instead belong far to the right side of the puzzle. I began to give those ideas some theological consideration.

I remember when I first closely inspected a piece of the puzzle found in 1 Corinthians 11:4–5: "Every man who prays or prophesies with his head covered dishonors his head. And every woman who prays or prophesies with her head uncovered dishonors her head—it is just as though her head were shaved." The indication here, that women prayed and prophesied in the Corinthian church, just did not have an interlocking tab to connect with my 1 Corinthians 14:34 piece of the puzzle in which women were not to speak *at all*. It seemed to me that just when I expected two pieces to fit together because they were, after all, penned by the same person and included in the same epistle, I found a contradiction. Paul appeared to make opposite points in chapters 11 and 14 in his letter to Corinth, and the explanations I was given (that chapter 11 did not connote a worship service, but 1 Corinthians 14 did) seemed to me, upon deeper investigation, to be forcing a fit that wasn't meant in the first place.

I then further scrutinized the piece of the puzzle from 1 Timothy 2, mentioned previously, and I saw that the wider context in the passage itself involved cultural issues that I hadn't fully considered before:

> Therefore I want the men everywhere to pray, lifting up holy hands without anger or disputing. I also want the women to dress modestly, with decency and propriety, adorning themselves, not with elaborate hairstyles or gold or pearls or expensive clothes, but with good deeds, appropriate for women who profess to worship God. A woman should learn in quietness and full submission. I do not permit a woman to teach or to assume authority over a man; she must be quiet. (1 Tim. 2:8–12)

It was obvious that the churches with which I was familiar did *not* encourage men to lift holy hands, nor did they prohibit women when it came to wearing gold or pearls, even though those were Paul's specific commands in this passage. These churches taught that Paul was making culturally specific points on those issues; they did not consider the way a woman learned or taught also to be cultural issues. The lines that were drawn bewildered me, and the puzzle simply wasn't coming together consistently.

As I looked more closely at the center of my puzzle, I often wanted to give up. It seemed I had some options in my attempt to configure my place in the body of Christ: find a way to be satisfied with the segment of the puzzle I had assembled thus far; with hierarchy in the center, throw all the pieces back into the box and start all over from scratch; or give up altogether and buy a secular puzzle for my life.

I didn't give up, although the mysterious ill-fitting puzzle pieces kept showing up in my box and began to outnumber those that did fit. I decided to keep the section I had arranged thus far, and I also began to arrange another part of the puzzle. I figured that when puzzled, it was best to begin where Scripture itself begins. In Genesis 1, I read that "God created human beings in his image, in the image of God he created them; male and female he created them" (v. 27, TNIV). As I went back to the very beginning of God's story, I did not find hierarchy in the creation account, although many certainly do. The Genesis narrative is about an invitation from God to human beings, inviting them into unity and kinship. This invitation is presented equally to both male and female. The community once perfectly experienced by Adam and Eve with the Father, the Son, and the Holy Spirit was broken early in the story, when humans fell for the serpent's lie, "You will not surely die." Choosing physical death, they also chose the death of perfect unity with God and one another, the death of all deaths. The broken world that resulted and God's covenant to heal that brokenness are chronicled in the story of Israel. God's plan was accomplished through a time in history in which hierarchy and fracture were a result of the death humans had chosen. God did not leave human beings in brokenness. Instead, we read a story in which God made a way to bring back to life what was dead.

I next inspected the puzzle pieces that came when God became a human on behalf of all humans. As I picked up the pieces of the puzzle that reflected Jesus' time on earth, I saw how Jesus looked at women like me. I noted that when Mary sat at the Lord's feet in Luke 10, listening to what he taught, she was commended for having made the better choice. I pictured myself kneeling in Mary's posture, and I imagined what it meant to receive the Lord's approval for my desire to learn in ways that perhaps brought disapproval in my culture, similar to Martha's indignation toward her sister Mary. I wondered if Martha was upset with Mary not only because she wasn't doing her share of the work but because she was taking part in full discipleship: sitting at the feet and learning from a rabbi, a role usually set aside for men. As I contemplated Jesus' words about Mary, I imagined what it would mean to hear him say to my sisters and brothers, ". . . [Y]ou are worried and upset about many things, but only one thing is needed. Sara has chosen what is better, and it will not be taken away from her."

I uncovered a puzzle piece in which Jesus himself counter-culturally commissioned a Samaritan woman as his witness: to be a missionary and teacher of her people. Even Jesus' disciples were surprised to find him talking with a Samaritan, a Samaritan *woman*, in fact. We forget the cultural gulfs between Jesus and that woman at the well, but she was called to testify boldly regardless of cultural expectations. With the outsider in John 4, I decided not to sip but to drink deeply of the water of life.

I then located pieces of the early church puzzle in which four daughters of the evangelist Philip prophesied (Acts 21), a woman, Phoebe, was a deacon in the church, and a woman, Junia, was named as great among the apostles. I observed that Priscilla was mentioned as a co-worker for Christ in the same way that her husband was a co-worker. I saw the names of Tryphena and Tryphosa and Persis, women who worked hard for the Lord (Rom. 16).

I saw that when it came to church life, our sons were included and mentored as Bible readers, communion servers, and money counters. Whether it's fair or not, I gathered from the boys' priority at church that daughters were second best. In Scripture, however, I saw daughters liberated as *full* children of God because of redemption that came through Jesus Christ and replaced the old Law of Moses. In John 1, I read a passage emphasizing that God does not play favorites among his children:

> Yet to all who received him, to those who believed in his name,
> he gave the right to become children of God—children born

> not of natural descent, nor of human decision or a husband's
> will, but born of God. . . . From the fullness of his grace we
> have all received one blessing after another. For the law was
> given through Moses; grace and truth came through Jesus
> Christ. (1 John 1:12–13; 16–17)

I ascertained that when the curtain of the temple was torn in two (Matt. 27:51, Mark 15:38, Luke 23:45), new fellowship with God was given to *all* because of what happened in Jesus Christ, the Son of God, erasing barriers that came as a result of the fall. When Jesus visited the temple, it was in the process of being extensively renovated by Herod. Herod apparently wanted to restore the temple to the splendor of Solomon's day, and a great amount of money was spent in the renovation. The historian Josephus explains to us that the temple reflected hierarchy, although nowhere in the Old Testament do we read that it was God's idea to establish the divisions of Herod's temple. First, on the lower level, was the Court of the Gentiles, where even moneychangers and livestock dealers could enter; the only restriction for that court was that menstruating women could not enter at all. Beyond that court, a high wall divided the Court of the Gentiles from the temple proper. The message of the wall was clear, as it included warnings written in Latin, Greek, and Hebrew: Gentiles were not to go beyond the Court of the Gentiles, and a penalty of death awaited those who trespassed.

After the Court of the Gentiles, Israelite worshipers ascended to the next level of the temple, the Court of the Women. Women did not go beyond this area, which was the likely site where Jesus, surrounded by the hustle and bustle of the crowds, zoned in on one true worshiper and spoke these words: "Truly I tell you, this poor widow has put in more than all the others. All these people gave their gifts out of their wealth, but she out of her poverty put in all she had to live on" (Luke 21:3–4).

Ritually pure Israelite men, who could leave the Court of the Women, entered the next level of the temple as they mounted a splendid spiral staircase and traversed a narrow hallway to enter the Court of the Israelites. This court surrounded the Court of the Priests, another echelon of hierarchy, containing the altar of sacrifice. I imagine women, staying behind in their court, standing on tippy-toes, peeking into the Court of Priests, hoping to see the sacrifices being made, but they could not enter this court themselves.

Even further into the temple was an inner room called the Holy of Holies, the most sacred dwelling of God. A fine, embroidered curtain separated the Holy of Holies from the Most Holy Place, where God dwelt, as nearly as God might dwell anywhere on earth (2 Chron. 3:14). The curtain represented a barrier between humans and God. This was not a curtain that a curious child might peer behind, for if someone carelessly went beyond the curtain into the Holy of Holies, that person would die. This curtain, known as a veil, featured embroidered cherubim who guarded the throne of God. The veil was made of linen and blue, purple, and scarlet yarn. Only the high priest could enter the Most Holy Place and speak the name of Yahweh one time a year, on the Day of Atonement.

With the layout of the temple in mind and the theological significance of the curtain considered, therefore, the passages that refer to the tearing of the curtain recorded in Matthew, Mark, and Luke's Gospels are significant for *all* people and *all* our relationships with each other as we relate to God.

> At noon, darkness came over the whole land until three in the afternoon. And at three in the afternoon Jesus cried out in a loud voice, "Eloi, eloi, lema sabachthani?" (which means "My God, my God, why have you forsaken me?").

> When some of those standing near heard this, they
> said, "Listen, he's calling Elijah." Someone ran, filled a
> sponge with wine vinegar, put it on a staff, and offered it
> to Jesus to drink. "Now leave him alone. Let's see if Elijah
> comes to take him down," he said.
>
> With a loud cry, Jesus breathed his last.
>
> The curtain of the temple was torn in two from top to
> bottom. And when the centurion, who stood there in front
> of Jesus, saw how he died, he said, "Surely this man was the
> Son of God!" (Mark 15:33–39)

It is through the life, death, and resurrection of Jesus, God's own Son, that
human relationships with God and one another are radically redefined.
It is through Jesus, the great high priest, that our hope is anchored in the
sanctuary behind the curtain, where Jesus entered on our behalf (Heb.
6:19–20). It is through Jesus that all are welcomed equally and without
hindrance into his presence, for he is our peace, having destroyed the
dividing wall of hostility (Eph. 2:14). We say with hope and peace, "Surely
this man was the Son of God," and it is through him that all human beings
may be children of God through faith. As Paul wrote:

> So, in Christ Jesus you are all children of God through faith,
> for all of you who were baptized into Christ have clothed
> yourselves with Christ. There is neither Jew nor Gentile,
> neither slave nor free, nor is there male and female, for you
> are all one in Christ Jesus. If you belong to Christ, then you
> are Abraham's seed, and heirs according to the promise."
> (Gal. 3:26–29)

The tearing of that curtain, recorded in the Synoptic Gospels, became
central in the topography of my puzzling process. The entire story of the

Bible, for all nations and all people, heads toward an invitation to inclusion, not exclusion.

I then discovered an important puzzle piece from Revelation 22 in the bottom of the box, and it came into focus as I held it over the puzzle I had so far:

> Then the angel showed me the river of the water of life.... On each side of the river stood the tree of life . . . and the leaves of the tree are for the healing of nations. No longer will there be any curse.... "Behold, I am coming soon! My reward is with me, and I will give to everyone according to what he has done. I am the Alpha and the Omega, the First and the Last, the Beginning and the End." (Rev. 22:1a, 2b–3a, 12–13)

All that occurred in the life, death, and resurrection of Jesus Christ served to overcome the repercussions of the fall; although the full results of that victory are yet to be fully known, Christians are called to work toward inclusion of all because all are one in the One who gives us identity, Jesus Christ.

I have spent my life trying, in the company of believers with whom God has placed me, to puzzle these scriptures—trying to figure out who God created us to be and what Scripture has to say about it. I'm still on the journey. Scripture continues to puzzle me, but now I feel blessed and challenged by my experience in Scripture rather than ashamed of what God is teaching me through it. When I get stuck on a difficult text, I try to remember how Jesus defined the most important commands, "Love the Lord your God with all your heart, soul, and mind. And love your neighbor as yourself." All the puzzling aspects of the Law and the Prophets hang on these two commands.

Hopefully, we've all been navigating Scripture in our lives—trying to figure out who God created us to be and what Scripture has to say about it, weighing all of it with what we've been taught. Inherently, this journey brings some peace and some confusion. That's how God designed it. Perhaps no one is given a puzzle with a picture included on the box; maybe that's God's invitation to life within the community of the Father, the Son, the Spirit, and the church.

chapter six | **beyond my own edges**

Life is like a puzzle, and God, with great mercy, has provided me with the Holy Spirit and with dear Christian brothers and sisters who are helping me develop my life puzzle (and I pray I am helping them in return). It turns out, you see, that the life puzzle I described in the previous chapter doesn't have straight, edge pieces to define an individual perimeter! There is no separate box of puzzle pieces for each believer. We are one in Christ, so the edges of my puzzle contain connecting points where the puzzles of other people connect to my own. Through the power of the Holy Spirit working in each of our lives, we function as a whole. It must be a beautiful picture for God to behold from above, even if we can't see it all yet.

The human relationship that has most provided connection for me is my marriage relationship with my husband, John. For more than twenty years I have lived in a Christian marriage that is not perfect, but one in which John and I both seek to be filled with the Spirit.

A passage that often comes up in discussion about gender roles in marriage and church life is found in Ephesians 5, where verse 22 is especially well known. "Wives, submit to your husbands as to the Lord." In

today's society, *submit* is not a popular word, as evidenced in the following transcript from the TV show *The West Wing*, which was popular a few
years ago. The show is set in the United States White House. Follow along
as characters President Bartlet and his wife Abbey discuss Ephesians 5:21
with White House aide Charlie, who asks, "How was church?"

> ABBEY: He feels the homily lacked panache.
>
> BARTLET: It did lack panache.
>
> ABBEY: It was a perfectly lovely homily on Ephesians
> 5:21. "Husbands, love your wives, as Christ
> loved the church and gave himself up
> for her."
>
> BARTLET: Yeah. She's skipping over the part that says,
> "Wives, be subject to your husbands as to
> the Lord, for a husband is the head of a wife
> as Christ is the head of the church."
>
> ABBEY: I do skip over that part.
>
> BARTLET: Why?
>
> ABBEY: Because it's stupid!
>
> BARTLET: You can't just trod out Ephesians, which
> he blew, by the way, it has nothing [to do]
> with husbands and wives, it's all of us. Saint
> Paul begins the passage, "Be subject to one
> another out of reverence to Christ."

This *West Wing* conversation illustrates the sensitivity in our culture to
the Ephesians 5 passage. I don't think Ephesians 5 is stupid, as Abbey
says, but I also don't agree with the perspective that it has nothing to
do with husbands and wives, as Bartlet says. Christians, however, must
realize that both reactions find resonance in our world. In our context, it
is tempting to call it stupid or explain it away. In our marriage, John and

I choose to celebrate the good news in the passage instead, bringing the core of its message into our time and place.

The sentiment "they lived happily ever after" is central to our fairy tales and romantic comedies, but "they submitted in holiness forever after" is not. My marriage makes me very happy, but there's much more to it than fairy tale happiness, something deeper that only comes through Christ. Gary Thomas writes in his book *Sacred Marriage* that marriage should be a profound opportunity to be made holy, to be sanctified as we are filled with the Spirit and live self-sacrificially with another person. He stresses that even though happiness is often emphasized as a goal of marriage, the goal of holiness is not always widely discussed.

Ephesians 5, however, contains just this advice—advice for the married couple about being filled with the Spirit. The passage is not primarily about marital happiness and compatibility. It's not primarily about the proper balance regarding who's in charge or how decisions will be made. It is about both partners being made holy, being filled with the Spirit.

In Ephesians 5, Paul offers advice about how wives and husbands may live in uniquely Christian relationships in which the gospel is good news for marriage. To understand what that good news is for households in our day, it helps to understand what it meant in Paul's day. Paul was advising early believers about how to be filled with the Spirit in the existing structure and context of Greco-Roman society of the first century, detailing how their households and relationships should be transformed because they had chosen to walk in the way of love, imitating Christ (Eph. 5:1–2).

I understand Paul's words about submission in 5:21 in light of the rest of the chapter, and in this way. First, Paul says in 5:1–2: Imitate Christ. Then, he warns those who are imitating Christ not to be unwise and live according to the flesh, but to be wise and take every opportunity to be filled with the Spirit (5:15–19). Then, Paul explains what being filled with the Spirit looks like in the marriage relationship (5:21–33).

In this passage about marriage, one of the scriptures most used in wedding ceremonies and to explain marriage relationships, translators have traditionally made what seems to some scholars to be an error in how they've divided paragraphs and sentences. To the untrained eye, the Greek scriptures look like one big, long, run-on sentence. Translators not only have decisions to make about what words to use when they translate, but they must also decide where to divide sentences and paragraphs.

In some translations, Ephesians 5:21, "Submit to one another out of reverence for Christ" is placed at the end of the paragraph, just after verse 20. In other translations, however, Ephesians 5:21 is placed apart from verse 20 and begins a new paragraph. The question is whether 5:21 is the conclusion of the previous section or the introduction to the new one. The placement of this one sentence makes a major difference in how we read instructions to husbands and wives, beginning in verse 22. The key verse is set apart below so that you may test each reading for yourselves, and I suggest that you consult different translations to see where the paragraph break has been made.

> Be very careful, then, how you live—not as unwise but as wise, making the most of every opportunity, because the days are evil. Therefore do not be foolish, but understand what the Lord's will is. Do not get drunk on wine, which leads to debauchery. Instead, be filled with the Spirit. Speak to one another with psalms, hymns and spiritual songs. Sing and make music in your heart to the Lord, always giving thanks to God the Father for everything, in the name of our Lord Jesus Christ. (verse 20)
>
> Submit to one another out of reverence for Christ. (verse 21)

Wives, submit to your husbands as to the Lord.
(verse 22)

For the husband is the head of the wife as Christ is the
head of the church, his body, of which he is the Savior. Now
as the church submits to Christ, so also wives should submit
to their husbands in everything. Husbands, love your wives,
just as Christ loved the church and gave himself up for her
to make her holy, cleansing her by the washing with water
through the word, and to present her to himself as a radiant
church, without stain or wrinkle or any other blemish, but
holy and blameless. In this same way, husbands ought to
love their wives as their own bodies. He who loves his wife
loves himself. (Eph. 5:15–28)

As explained above, our interpretation of this passage is shaped by decisions about where verse 21 goes. Does it conclude the ideas about life
in the Spirit in the former verses, or does it introduce the ideas about
marriage in the latter passage? I follow a good number of scholars and
translators who place it at the beginning of a new paragraph, because in
the original Greek, the word *submit* does not actually exist in verse 22. It
reads, "Submit to one another out of reverence to Christ. Wives, to your
husbands as to the Lord." Verse 22 must receive its verb from the previous sentence in verse 21, so it makes good sense that the two sentences
should be grouped together. Read in this way, verse 21 introduces and
summarizes Paul's advice to both husbands and wives so that both view
their marriage roles in light of their discipleship.

Paul's writing is to be admired in this section. He tells readers that he
will move into a section in which he discusses submission to one another
out of reverence to Christ (verse 21). He begins with wives, moves on to
husbands, and beautifully ties the marriage relationship to the mystery

of unity with Christ and the church (the consistent theme to which Paul always returns in his epistles). The placement of verse 21 is not the only consideration in interpretation of the passage, but it is an important one.

It's also important to consider how Paul's first readers understood these words. Though there were pockets in which women were empowered in Greco-Roman life, the idea that men and women might be equal partners in marriage would not have been conceivable; that's a modern concept. The husband's role as master of his household was clear and undisputed. It was clear that his family served him and his gods. Some husbands might be kind, but others might be hurtful. Regardless of his manner, others in the household by law could not address grievances in any legal way. It stands to reason that the women Paul addressed in Ephesians 5 could not have responded as Abbey Bartlet's character did, and told her husband his advice was "stupid." Paul's message about households was originally addressed to marriage partners in a context quite unlike that of Western marriages today.

It helps when we look at the Ephesians 5 passage to understand that this kind of societal instruction was common in discourse of the day. The social categories of the Greco-Roman world were influenced by the writings of Greek philosophers. Aristotle, for example, penned codes concerning social structure. He began with this line: "The male is by nature superior, and the female inferior; and the one rules, and the other is ruled; this principle of necessity extends to all mankind . . . ." Aristotle's code is only one example among many others of teaching about household relationships. What is helpful is to look at other household codes of the day and to notice what Paul said that was expected and longstanding and what was unexpected and new.

The difference that is immediately evident is that household codes rarely addressed men, making their absolute power clear. The codes were primarily directed toward subordinates in the household: wives, children, and slaves. The codes were certain; subordinates were to submit to the master of the household.

So when Paul addressed husbands in his version of household codes, it was notable. He was deviating from the norm. The good news transforms understanding of power because Jesus transformed understanding of power. Paul was explaining what it meant when the Spirit was at work, creating reciprocity between husbands and wives, fathers and children, masters and slaves. Those in positions of superiority received detailed advice, even more than those without power. Those without power were not ignored—they were called to transformation as well—but the prominence of advice to husband, father, and master would have been potent to readers of the time.

Interpretations of this text are disputable, as evidenced by the variety of interpretations of the passage throughout history. I can't presume to include all viewpoints here, but what I can do is share what I understand the passage to be saying, especially concerning the marriage relationship. In essence, I understand Ephesians 5 to advise wives to imitate Christ and be filled with the Spirit. Their relationships should be transformed. They were not told to cease submitting to their husbands, but they were called to submit differently because of Christ. They were not to obey simply because they had no choice, perhaps even with secret resentment. Instead, they should submit out of reverence to Christ, whose Spirit filled them.

Then Paul chose to highlight his advice to husbands in light of the whole gospel story. He told them to love their wives, not just to further a family line, to run a household, or to prove that their wives are their possessions. Husbands were challenged to define power in light of how Christ defined power. Christ, who was in very nature God, did not consider equality with God something to be used to his own advantage but took the nature of a servant and sacrificed himself on the cross (Phil. 2).

Paul clearly challenged husbands to redefine their role in terms of Christ's sacrificial love.

With his advice, Paul did not dismantle everything about the structure of Christian households in Greco-Roman society. It was quite possible to live as disciples within the basic structures of the ancient world. Paul's advice came within those structures, while at the same time challenging them. Because a complete change of structure would have been disgraceful in their context, he applied the good news to the context of the day.

When we read Ephesians, understanding the broad Greco-Roman world is vital. Yet there's a difference in understanding a situation and replicating it. Modern households and societal structures look nothing like Greco-Roman households. Today, women and men have the same rights to education, to participation in democratic society as full voters, and to serve in almost every way in public society. All of this would have been totally foreign to Paul's world. That doesn't mean that we call his advice stupid after church on Sunday. We do have to ask, however, what brings shame upon Christianity in our day and time. Paul gave his advice with that concern in mind in Ephesians, so we must do the same.

When John and I discern how to live in our marriage as Christians in the twenty-first century, we ask what it means to be filled with the Spirit in our household and to have our relationship transformed through Christ in our day and time. Inspired texts are living testimonies that continue to speak to new circumstances through time. I am not a woman in the first-century world, nor does John occupy that world. But this text speaks no less to our lives because it calls us to discipleship in our marriage and to submit to one another out of reverence to Christ in our current circumstance. And that has resulted in a marriage of mutual submission.

The lesson of Ephesians 5 says to us: John and Sara, your household is to be in the process of being filled with the Spirit. You should submit to one another out of reverence to Christ. Sara, submit to John as if serving the Lord. John, love Sara as Christ loves the church. Outdo one another in submission to one another. Both of you, imitate Jesus' definition of power in your own day and time.

Discussions about Ephesians 5 often turn to who will make hard decisions when a couple can't agree on something. I don't think Paul was primarily addressing decision-making. Although I cannot say that we've never faced difficult decisions, I can honestly say John and I have never come to a point where we couldn't make a decision together. We base our decisions on gifting, personality, and background. Sometimes we follow my lead, but other times we follow John's lead. It has not been perfect, but it's been possible through the power of the Spirit. For us, it's not about who's the master of the household; it's about how our marriage may reflect good news here and now.

My marriage, an experience with John of defining power through the lens of the good news, has influenced my thinking about church. When I talk about husband and wife and two being one flesh, it's "a profound mystery—but I am talking about Christ and the church" (Eph. 5:32). Paul tells us that transformation of relationships is a mystery that is not understood in a world that doesn't know Christ. Within the church, transformation of relationships should be clear throughout time and culture.

In researching this passage, I ran across the *Priscilla Papers* which connects intimately to my marriage with John. When explaining that husbands and wives were not viewed as equals in Greco-Roman society, Gordon Fee points out that equality was seen in who ate together. Those who were equal ate together, and those who were unequal did not share meals. It was not considered honorable to eat with non-equals, and a woman almost never joined her husband and his friends at meals. If she did, she didn't recline with them but sat on a bench at the end of the group and was expected to leave when the conversation took a public turn.

Imagine the revolutionary significance of shared meals in early Christianity! Those who had previously been unequal were made equal in Christ. Slaves shared meals with masters. Gentiles ate with Pharisees. The poor ate with the rich. Wives ate with husbands. In Christ's meal, people were no longer pitted against people. Transformation of relationships made the structures of equality and inequality ultimately irrelevant because power was completely redefined by the example of Christ.

Sharing the common meal of Christ is especially personal in my marriage because of an incident on a Sunday evening a few years ago. Our family was on the way to a small gathering that was designed specifically as a communion meal. The group wanted the communion meal to be experienced beyond a rushed moment of eating a tiny cracker and taking a little sip of juice and to be more like the experience of a full meal, in the example of the New Testament church. We were looking forward to the experience with friends, but on the way there, John and I got into an argument. It quickly went from a cross conversation to a genuine argument. We raised our voices beyond our typical spats. Neither of us can remember what we argued about, but we remember it was not something we handled well. Our kids were sitting in the back seat in complete silence. By the time we arrived at our destination, we weren't speaking at all.

We started to get out of the car, and in that moment, John embodied the good news for our family. He said, "Stop. Wait. I can't go in there, pretend everything is okay, and take communion like this." He then apologized for his part in the argument, asked the kids and me to forgive him, and led a family prayer. We didn't solve the argument in that moment, and his prayer didn't fix everything. But later, when we came to the moment of sharing Christ's meal as a family, I knew that my husband had shown me that the meal is about bringing people together in confession, submission, and reciprocity. Sharing the meal of Christ radically bridges divides.

John doesn't get his way all the time. I don't get my way all the time. John isn't always the one who leads in confession and apology; sometimes I do. We don't live in a happily ever after fairy tale, but we are being filled with the Spirit as we live in the kingdom of God. The fruits of the Spirit—love, joy, peace, patience, kindness, goodness, faithfulness, gentleness, and self-control—are growing in our household. A shared meal among us reflects a transformation of power in relationship as our world sees it.

Marriage has long been tied to the communion meal. As part of marriage services in the early church, the fulfillment of marriage by two Christians was sharing the communion meal. Matrimony received its seal through inclusion of this central act of the community. The Orthodox Church continues this practice of the early church today, and at some point in history they began to place crowns on the heads of the bride and groom as part of the marriage ceremony. The rite of crowning expresses the entrance of the two individuals as one into the church—into the kingdom.

Alexander Schmemann explains in his book, *For the Life of the World*, that the crowns of the marriage ceremony proclaim a message: This marriage is the beginning of a small kingdom that can be like the true kingdom. The love of the couple, in their unity and covenant with one another, will in some small way proclaim the love of God's kingdom. The crowns the couple wears will remind them to identify with a crown of thorns, choosing a marriage that constantly crucifies its own selfishness. Instead of idolizing and serving their own happiness, they take up the cross of Jesus and together give their marriage for the sake of the kingdom of God. After their crowning, the bride and groom seal their marriage in Christ by joining in the Eucharist, joining hands and following the priest in a procession around the table of the wine and bread. The Orthodox practice reminds us as Paul did: It's a mystery, but when we talk about a husband and wife, we are talking about Christ and the church.

Husbands and wives, as they are uniquely connected in God's big puzzle, are called to surrender to the direction of Ephesians 5: "Submit to one another out of reverence for Christ." Both the controlling husband who mandates his power and the progressive wife who considers submission to be stupid are worlds away from the intent of Ephesians 5. We are invited to fellowship around a table that transforms our relationships and connects our life puzzles mysteriously. And that's good news for husbands, wives, and the whole church.

part three | **that's not what i've always been taught**

chapter seven | **who do you think you are?**

When my husband and I were living as missionaries in Uganda, East Africa, I once taught a Bible study series about women in the Bible. With sisters in Wankonge village, I studied Sarah, the princess, the mother of nations. We studied Miriam, the sister of Moses and worship leader of Israel. I taught about Mary, the mother of Jesus, and about those two opposites, Mary and Martha. Women in the Bible: It was a good series for women in Uganda.

After several weeks, I decided to review what we had learned so far in the series. As I traversed the pothole maze to Wankonge, I mentally reviewed the local Lusoga vocabulary for several questions I wanted to ask the women. I had some really good questions about our study of women in the Bible.

I didn't get past the first one.

My first question was, "Which woman in our series about women do you like more than all the others—who is your favorite?" The women discussed the question among themselves a bit. In contrast to Western culture, when a question is asked of a group, no one tends to hold up a hand and say, "Pick me! Pick me!" Instead, the question receives communal attention and is given a communal answer. As the women chatted in Lusoga, and I tried to follow along with my less-than-impressive language skills, I eventually saw eyebrows raise in agreement over one woman's suggestion. Heads nodded in agreement to her favorite woman, so then she turned to me and said:

"The woman we like best in all the Bible is Bathsheba."

Bathsheba! I thought.

"Bathsheba?"

Inwardly, I wanted to argue with their answer. First of all, I wanted to point out that Bathsheba was not even part of *my* series on women in the Bible. We had learned about Bathsheba in the previous series when we studied King David. Bathsheba was not one of the women in the Bible I had chosen to highlight as a woman to emulate. She was, after all, a character in a sketchy story in Israelite history. Couldn't they see the scarlet letter "A" on Bathsheba's tunic? She was ultimately a party to the downfall of the great King David. Frankly, she was not one of *my* favorite characters. I wanted to say all of this to the women.

But I was a good missionary that day.

Instead, I said, "Lwaki (why?)." "Why do you like Bathsheba best?"

The conversation that followed is one I cherish.

The women shared with me that they liked Bathsheba because they could see their own lives in her story. For example, the way they explained it, Bathsheba had little personal choice in her life. The way they envisioned the sensational soap opera, Bathsheba went where she was told to go, and she was with the men in her life because the men said she should be with them. She didn't get to choose who she was with based on love or preference. Some of the women in our circle that day had marriages that reflected that kind of situation.

After their first reason for liking Bathsheba, I understood her appeal a bit better. Next they shared that they could identify with Bathsheba because she was a "co-wife"—a wife among other wives. She was a wife in a polygamous situation, and some of the women in the group lived in polygamous households or had grown up in them. If they did not yet share their husbands with other women, they suspected that it might happen to them when they became old or if they did not give birth to children. The women told me that they admired Bathsheba because even in a polygamous marriage, she was honorable. She raised a good son despite her circumstances, and they pointed out that she was David's favorite wife. She was a role model to them. They disclosed something that was foreign to my experience but realistic in theirs: "If you are going to be a co-wife, you want to be the favorite co-wife."

Our Bible study then took a turn that pierced my heart as my companions told me that they were most drawn to Bathsheba because her baby died. They could identify with Bathsheba's grief because the reality is that one in five babies born in Uganda will not live to see a fifth birthday. The women in Wankonge knew what it meant to beg God to spare a sick baby only to have the child die in their arms. They knew what it was to wail at the graveside as their precious child was covered with dirt. And so, as Bathsheba grieved, they grieved with her.

And they liked her.

Finally, one of the women, Goretti, revealed the depth of her grasp on the good news of the gospel. She said, "I like Bathsheba because she was brought very low. She was humbled because everyone was watching her suffering. But God raised her up again when she was given a healthy child who became a great king. She was like Jesus, who was humbled and then raised up as a king. When I am low, I know that God will not leave me there to suffer; he will raise me up like he raised Jesus up from the cross."

As I listened to my Ugandan friends discuss Bathsheba that day, I began to think, *I like Bathsheba!* My understanding of this woman from ancient times and of the Scriptures that testify to her part in the epic story of God (including the genealogy of the Messiah) was forever changed because of the perspective of wise women in a rural village deep in Uganda.

The experience made me want to learn more about how Bathsheba has been interpreted in other times and places, and in that process I discovered a rich history of biblical interpretation in the work of artists in European art tradition. For many, with her legendary beauty, Bathsheba was the perfect character through whom to explore the timeless seduction of femininity and the scandal of a great man falling because of his weakness for a woman. As artists painted Bathsheba, they interpreted her through their own interpretive processes and translated the story in their time and place. Through the centuries, since the day she bathed on that rooftop, Bathsheba has often been depicted as a temptress, intentionally bathing in David's view to seduce him, and she was frequently painted holding a mirror, vainly taken by her own beauty. Italian painter Sebastiano Ricci's (1659–1734) *Bathsheba* is an example of an interpretive judgment upon Bathsheba as she is shown preparing herself for David's gaze while looking into a mirror held by a servant. Alternately, Rembrandt's work, *Bathsheba with King David's Letter,* currently displayed in the Louvre in Paris, stands in contrast to others because he chose to go beyond former interpretations of Bathsheba as temptress and explore with empathy Bathsheba's difficult moral dilemma when David sent for her.

We will never know exactly how the bathing episode took place, but we can agree that it is a broken story God can use to teach surprising lessons about redemptive work. It's surprising, don't you think, that God raises up the brokenhearted? It's surprising, don't you think, that God forgives sin like that of King David? It's surprisingly good news, don't you think, that God lifted up Jesus Christ? Good news inherently involves a measure of surprise.

Matthew chose to begin his good news with this very theme of surprise. We might think we should skip over the genealogy if we want to experience surprise. Maybe we should go straight to the shocking part about the virgin being with child. But Matthew emphasizes surprise in the genealogy in purposeful ways. "This is a genealogy. . . ." A genealogy? So-and-so begat so-and-so who begat so-and-so. I have to confess that the way I may have read biblical genealogies in the past, they were *boring* news, not *good* news. But that's my fault, not Matthew's! The news that God's kingdom comes on earth as it is in heaven is the very best news we will ever hear.

Our ancestors in faith in the early church would not have heard Matthew's good news with a humdrum attitude. The good news of the gospel for them was about what God was doing to overturn the world's expectations, and they saw their relationships with God and each other as part of it. They, like my friend Goretti, saw how God was raising up unexpected people to join in proclaiming the good news. The stories of dead ancestors came alive in surprising ways when they looked at the genealogy with their new understandings of what happened in Jesus Christ.

Inspecting the genealogy for examples of those reversals, we have to admit that it's a bit of a surprise that Jesus is from the tribe of Judah. We can think back on the stories of Israel and ask—wait a minute, why wasn't Jesus from Joseph's tribe? Joseph was clearly the superior bundle of grain. Instead, we get Judah, the very Judah who mistreated his daughter-in-law, Tamar, a woman uniquely described as righteous in the Old Testament. It's notable that God does not always work through the people we think are the obvious candidates.

According to Levirate law, Judah had not done what was right for Tamar, his twice-widowed daughter-in-law. He should have arranged for the family line to be carried out through Tamar by sending his third son to marry her. According to Deuteronomy, a woman in this situation could go to the elders and say, "My husband's brother refuses to carry on his brother's name. He will not fulfill the duty of a brother-in-law to me." If after counsel the brother still refused to marry her, the widow would go to him in the presence of the elders, take off one of his sandals, spit in his face, and say, "This is what is done to the man who will not build up his brother's family line." The family would then be known as the "unsandaled" (Deut. 25:5–10). As strange as it sounds to us today, Tamar likely had options of that sort, but instead she decided that perhaps Judah, the father, was the one to be held responsible. So she disguised herself as a prostitute and seduced him so that she could have a child, as was her right according to the law. She kept his staff and seal, his identification papers of the day, as collateral for her services.

When Judah later found out Tamar was pregnant, quite ironically, he planned to have her killed on the grounds of adultery. And then, in a moment of theater, Tamar produced the down payment she had been given as evidence that Judah was the father of the child. One of my students recently referred to this moment as the first ever episode of the scandalous TV show *Maury Povich: Who's Your Daddy?* Judah's staff and seal proved she was not the one to be judged in the situation.

Women weren't even routinely included in Jewish genealogies, yet a woman, a Gentile woman at that, who pretended to be a prostitute turned out to be the heroic, righteous ancestor in this story. To top it off, the chastened character, Judah, was central to the story of Jesus. We can be sure that Matthew's audience knew this story and perceived the surprising connection to the gospel as the genealogy was read. This story brings good news of radical, surprising redefinition of relationships in Jesus Christ.

It's especially intriguing that when Matthew continues in the genealogy and gets to the story of David and Bathsheba, he chooses not to use Bathsheba's name in his account, instead using her murdered husband's name. He refers to other women by name: Tamar, Rahab, and Ruth. He refers to Bathsheba, though, by saying, "David was the father of Solomon, whose mother had been Uriah's wife." Ouch! When narrating the genealogy of Jesus the Messiah, Matthew decisively chose to call attention to the fact that David took a woman who was not his wife. He emphasized instead, a Gentile, Uriah the Hittite, the principled character in the story. In this short line of the genealogy, Matthew aired Israel's dirty laundry for all to see and pointed out that the expected virtuous character is not always the one a worldly perspective might anticipate when it comes to the good news he's relaying. A close reading of the genealogy reminds us that God's redemptive work includes, and in fact has always pointed toward, inclusion of saint and sinner, Jew and Gentile, male and female, expected and unexpected.

As we examine the genealogy, we see that God frequently chose to work toward redemption of the world through people who in the eyes of that very world were

> second best (Leah's son over Rachel's son?),
> unknown (who is Eliud, or is it Elihud?),
> a sinner (David: adulterer, murderer, liar, saint?),
> outsiders (Rahab, a harlot, and Ruth, a Moabitess?),
> unexpected (Mary and Joseph from nowheresville-
> Nazareth of all places, not to mention unmarried?)

It turns out that a genealogy can be riveting when we know the stories behind it, and a list of Old Testament names can be full of good news of God's surprising redefinitions of power and reversals of expectation when we have eyes to see.

As I write about ancestry, I am reminded that researching one's genealogy has become of great interest in recent years. For a hobby that revolves around dead people, it attracts a large number of people. According to the United States Census Bureau, over 80 million Americans are actively researching their family histories. The TV show *Who Do You Think You Are?* highlights this growing interest in ancestry. In each episode, a celebrity learns about an intriguing ancestor, one who was born a slave but died a business owner, or was a scoundrel who did jail time, or was accused of witchcraft in the Salem witch trials. The show makes it a point to highlight how the celebrities begin to think of themselves anew because of the stories of their ancestors. Our families, even our distant relatives from generations past, tell us who we are.

Matthew's genealogy functions similarly for believers: This is who we are, and that tells us something about the good news!

Matthew's genealogy invites us to join what God is doing in the kingdom of heaven, regardless of noble lineage, gender, or religious pedigree. Who better to explain the invitation to God's upside-down kingdom than a suspected tax collector? Matthew says in essence: These people— Abraham, Tamar, Ruth, David, Eliud—are the kind of people God can use, the whole lot of them, warts and all, whether Jew or Gentile, whether male or female.

The kingdom of heaven into which we are invited insists upon radical, surprising redefinition of relationships and reversals of expectations, even the relationships between men and women. We pray as Jesus taught us, ". . . your kingdom come, your will be done on earth as it is in heaven" (Matt. 6:10), and in praying this prayer, we believe that relationships in the kingdom on earth are being made to look like the ones in heaven.

That's where we start when we read Matthew's genealogy, and it's where we start when we read the Bible, with an understanding of the good news. It's how we know who we are in Christ; we're the ones who continually surprise the world with radical, surprising, kingdom relationships. And we proclaim and live that good news until the very end of the age.

chapter eight | **that's not what i've always been taught**

I'm a part of an intergenerational group of women that ranges in age from our twenties to our eighties. We meet regularly to encourage and pray for one another. We are women from all walks of life—a tax consultant, college professors, a social worker, a public relations consultant, an executive assistant, a fitness expert, a director of a nonprofit organization, a preschool teacher, mothers, grandmothers, and friends. The members of our group have shared life through cancer, brain surgery, divorce, infertility, birth, adoption, weddings, deaths of spouses, loss of jobs, and job accomplishments. We meet regularly and share our lives. That's our goal, our mission statement: We share life. We support one another, love one another, listen to one another, cry with one another, and laugh with one another. I've learned so much about how to be *me* from all of them.

For years, I prayed for a community of women like this; God answered that request in a big way with my share group. There's no way I can describe what this group means to me and what an answer to prayer they are. Perhaps detailing a day in the life of our group is better than any description I can give.

We got together one particular week for Nola's birthday. Nola is the glue that holds our group together. Her grandchildren call her "Gra-Nola." I love that! Gra-Nola describes her so well. She's sort of nutty, spicy, sweet, and rich all at the same time. She is one of the most active, holistic people I've ever known despite having multiple sclerosis. One might expect her to be physically disabled, but Nola lives the big life. She lives large in all aspects of life: the physical, the spiritual, the emotional. She's Gra-Nola, a mix of all the good stuff.

Birthday parties for people like Nola are just bound to be special. When we gathered at a local restaurant, we were thankful that there were not many other people in our small dining room because we were *loud*. We have the ability to all talk at the same time but to inherently know when to stop and listen to one person when the need arises. We know how to go from silly and irreverent to serious and holy all within one unspoken moment.

In one of those group conversations, Heidi was telling me that her teenage daughter, Hillary, asked her, "Mom, what's an activist?"

"An activist is someone who really believes in a cause and is willing to stand up to represent it," Heidi told her daughter.

Hillary told Heidi, "I'm an activist, then."

"What are you an activist for?" her mom asked.

"I'm an activist for women in church," said Hillary. "I think it's wrong how women are treated at church."

As Heidi and I were having this conversation, it was one of those moments when the other conversations became quiet, and everyone at the table was listening to Heidi's story about Hillary. Heidi, who grew up in our church fellowship her entire life, as did all of us at the table, was sharing this story with pride in who her daughter is, but also with the edge of emotion that comes with the topic.

Joanne, the oldest member of our group, whose wisdom is respected among us, said, "This new young generation of women will not sit back

chapter eight | that's not what i've always been taught

and do what my generation did. We stayed quiet and didn't ask questions, even if we thought of them. My granddaughters don't understand why we were quiet about this. They will not be quiet."

Paula said, "Oh, we never heard anything about women participating in leadership at church except for 'women are to be silent in the church,' and we didn't question it. Even if we thought it, we were quiet. It's just how things were."

Heidi replied, "Growing up in the seventies, what I heard was that women can teach groups of boys and girls until they reach fourth grade Sunday school because boys under fourth grade were not likely to be baptized. But once they were baptized, women couldn't even teach them in Sunday school anymore because that would be having authority over a baptized male. I just didn't question that. It all seemed to make sense because it's what we were taught and what everyone seemed to agree about."

Nola added, "I was raised to believe that women should not do *anything* at church because the Bible says women are to be silent, and even though my mind is open to the idea of doing more now, I still can't leave all that behind me. I think it is about the new generation and us supporting them."

"But Nola," I said, "You have so much to share. It's not too late for you. I think the best way you can support the young generation is by stepping out and speaking up yourself. The church needs to see wise women doing that."

Nola's response was to tell a story we already knew, but it's one of those stories we can hear again and again. We know the story so well that we anticipate the cues for when to laugh, and that's half the fun of the story. She said, "I remember when I started to think differently about this issue. I had been talking to my niece about her faith, and eventually she asked me to baptize her. I thought of baptizing someone as a role of authority for men only."

My first reaction was to say, "Oh, honey, why don't you get Uncle Bob [Nola's husband] to baptize you?"

"I don't want Uncle Bob," she said.

"Then why don't you ask Rob [Nola's son] to baptize you?"

"I don't want Rob to baptize me. I want *you* to baptize me, Aunt Nola." (Laughter and ooohs and aahhs.)

"What could I do but baptize her?" said Nola. "So I went into that big cold lake where she wanted to be baptized, and my niece had a broken leg and a huge cast all wrapped up in plastic. But, that didn't stop us, and when I baptized her, it was one of the best moments of my life. I started thinking differently about women leading at church because of that experience."

This group of women rarely talks about gender concerns at church. Besides me (and Heidi's daughter Hillary, apparently), we aren't a bunch of activists who talk about church politics when we get together. We're just normal women, full of problems and fears and joys and celebration (sometimes all in the same night). We are women, all in love with Jesus and his body of believers.

Being a part of a close intergenerational group affords opportunities for older women to teach younger women; their wisdom helps put life into perspective. On my recent forty-third birthday, I received a birthday card from Joanne that said, "You are a wonderful young woman." It puts my birthdays in perspective that my older friend still sees me as a young woman. The mature women in our group take the responsibility of sharing their wisdom seriously, but something else they take seriously is openness to looking at things from diverse perspectives. We don't agree on all our topics of discussion, but this is a healthy group where we can disagree on important matters but end our conversations with shared prayer and unity.

A sentence that often arises in our intergenerational conversations about the Bible is "that's not what we've always been taught." There are different ways that sentence could be construed. "That's not what I've always been taught, so let's not discuss it." "That's not what I've been taught, so it makes me nervous or fearful." "That's not what we've always been taught, but I'm open to considering other points of view and continually rethinking what I've been taught." The attitude in my share group is found in the latter sentiment.

An important aspect of my church heritage I celebrate is that our members read and know the Bible. We're familiar with the stories and even have local competitions called "Bible Bowl," in which young people compete in a Bible version of the TV game show *Jeopardy*. Churches of Christ have always loved Scripture fiercely, prioritizing the view that we must go to Scripture ourselves, rather than accepting creeds and interpretations written by others. Founders of our movement stressed local autonomy for congregations that should read Scripture as communities of believers and discern together how to live out the gospel. We go to the Bible rather than depending on clergy to interpret for us. It's when we get stuck accepting what we've always been taught, without engaging it anew in an ongoing process, that we lose touch with our heritage.

I became a person of the Book because I was raised in a group that encouraged me to read for myself. My devotion to the Book is the result of a Bible-centered tradition. Now, however, I tend to read the Bible from a perspective that is not common in my heritage, and that's why I come to conclusions about gender roles other than the ones I was taught.

As I have immersed myself in Scripture, I have seen that the very phenomenon of Scripture guides me in how to read it. It seems to me that the Bible itself, in the very method through which God chose to give it, illustrates that we are to read and re-think its message in new ways in new times and places. In his book *The Blue Parakeet*, Scot McKnight illustrates how this took place throughout the biblical story, including both Hebrew Scriptures and the New Testament:

God spoke in Abraham's days in Abraham's ways (walking
between severed animals)
Moses' days in Moses' ways (law and ceremony)
David's days in David's ways (royal policies)
Isaiah's days in Isaiah's ways (walking around nude for a
few years)
Ezra's days in Ezra's ways (divorcing Gentile spouses)
Jesus' days in Jesus' ways (intentional poverty)
Peter's days in Peter's ways (strategies for living under
an emperor)
John's days in John's ways (dualistic language—light
and dark)

Adaptability and development are woven into the very fabric of the Bible. From beginning to end, there is a pattern of adopting and adapting. If we attempt to foist one person's days and ways on everyone's days and ways, we quench the Holy Spirit. Can we be biblical if we fail to be as adaptable as the Bible itself—only for our day? Is this messy? Sometimes it is. Was the Jerusalem council messy? Yes, it was. Did they discern what to do for that time? Yes, they did. Was it permanent for all time, for everyone, always, everywhere? No.

All genuine biblical faith takes the gospel message and "incarnates" it in a context.

McKnight's words remind us that God chose revelation that includes a story of interaction with humanity through a wide-angle lens, not at one particular time and place or even through one person. The Bible was thousands of years in the making. Perhaps that's because one small time period did not best encompass God's relationship with humanity. God sanctioned more than forty authors, who were under the guidance of the Holy Spirit, to communicate a vast story that stretches across cultures, times, and places. Perhaps that's because just one author's perspective is contradictory of who God is. Those authors used varying literary genres: poetry, song, story, historical records, *even* dialogue between two lovers, *even* long genealogies, *even* visions of future events. Perhaps that's because one genre just would not do. When Jesus Christ, the ultimate revelation of God, lived as a human being, this good news was penned by four different writers, Matthew, Mark, Luke, and John, perhaps because one point of view directed to only one audience, just would not do.

When God, who cannot be contained in a book, is made known as fully as human beings can understand and explain in words, it takes all kinds of approaches to even get close to describing the mystery, the story, and the intentions of God. The idea of reducing the will of God to snippets from one time and place goes against the very collection of documents we hold as divine revelation.

God could have chosen a different approach. A drama with so much variety and so many players isn't the only way. A checklist might be nice, or perhaps an edict might be clearer. A rulebook might give us the definitive answers we seek. A map showing how to find God would have been greatly helpful; a question-and-answer interview might have allowed humans to mine God for clarifications to our queries.

The reality is that God did not choose revelation through any of those means. In the chosen method, God is an active participant in relationship with people. As we read the Bible, we see that God's role is not that of a scientist managing robots. Neither is God a frustrated artist who left an incomplete work and chose to start an altogether different one. Throughout the biblical testimonies, God is an involved character who loves relentlessly, judges fairly, and joins wholly in ongoing relationship with creation. The Bible itself has a "to be continued" ending, and God is to be understood as continuing in the action of the drama. God still partners with people today in an ongoing story of renewal.

Early Christians knew that they were living in relationship with God in the continuing story. James Brownson, in his book *Speaking the Truth in Love*, challenges me to see that Christians in the New Testament celebrated the way the movement crossed cultural boundaries and was planted in new places in fresh ways. Ancient traditions, such as which foods or days were appropriate for eating, were being renegotiated as they moved forward. These were things that the people of God had laid down their lives to defend, and now they were suddenly called to another reality. Even circumcision, the ritual God gave Abraham, was no longer required in this new and fresh thing God was doing in Jesus. Early Christians expected the good news "to be continued," not confined to one place and time. So when we lose our imagination for a fresh new vision of the good news in our time and place, we do not understand the early church. Each context in which the good news was shared required a fresh vision for what it meant to be the Christian church in that time and place. Good News brought a fresh wind of hope for ongoing movement toward new creation.

Remembering that we are also in that "to be continued" time period is essential when we read Scripture. The good news is still on the move today. It's fundamental to the gospel that there are fresh understandings available to us as we live in God's story.

As believers mutually seek to enter this vast story of God and to live as one in Christ by God's grace, we must respect what we've been taught by generations who lived before us. Living in community demands that we respect the perspectives of Christians before and after us. Traditions in faith we are given by our mothers and fathers are important, not to be thrown out on a whim, for these traditions revive themselves season after season. Karl Paul Donfried said:

> The one thing the New Testament forbids us to do is to treat
> it as a static document to be used as a set of proof-texts for

> instant solutions to complex and controversial contempo-
> rary problems. To misuse the New Testament in this way
> is to deny its dynamic character and to fail to realize that
> the Word has to be applied in a specific context. . . . A static
> interpretation of the New Testament is dependent on a
> frozen Christology.

The story of Jesus is not frozen. It is a story of incarnation and can be embodied in every culture and period of time; it's that process Christians join. We must collectively (this is not about an individual) discern the intent behind the teaching that was handed to us and how it contributes in effectively proclaiming the good news of Jesus Christ in our time and place.

In that mindset of respect for one another and life in Jesus, we under-take the discernment process about how to proclaim the good news where we are. This discernment process is a daunting task, one that requires time *and prayer* and study *and prayer* and energy *and prayer* and patience *and prayer* and wisdom *and prayer and prayer and prayer*! It could seem easier to achieve community in Christ by simply accepting what we've always been taught and maintaining interpretations we've been given rather than living in dynamic relationship with God and one another, but static interpretations contradict the very nature of the good news. The good news itself demands fresh reading in ongoing motion, and in that dynamic process we receive the authority of God in our time and place. N. T. Wright wrote about tradition and Scripture in his book *Scripture and the Authority of God:*

> To affirm "the authority of scripture" is precisely not to say,
> "We know what scripture means and don't need to raise
> any more questions." It is always a way of saying that the
> church in each generation must make fresh and rejuvenated
> efforts to understand scripture more fully and live by it

more thoroughly, even if that means cutting across cher-
ished traditions.

This applies not least when the traditions in question
refer to themselves as "biblical." There are always some who
are ready, on hearing a new interpretation, to search the
scriptures afresh to see if these things are so (Acts 17:11).
But there are always others whose reactions to any new pro-
posal is to insist that since great preachers and teachers of
old have said what a particular passage means, there can be
nothing to add—and that even an attempt to say something
new is somehow impious or arrogant.

What does it look like when we read anew in changing context? That's
exactly what early disciples of Jesus wanted to know. What does it look
like when the kingdom of heaven is on the move? That's exactly what early
believers wanted to know, and as believers today, that is what my share
group seeks as well. Moreover, it's what this book is about. When it comes
to women serving in church ministries, how do we faithfully navigate our
stories, our times, and our situations? The gospel must be incarnated in
our days and our ways.

I sit around a table with my share group in these days, and we partake
in this ancient tradition of wrestling with where we all fit into the story of
God. We are an incarnated presence, asking each other how Jesus resides
among us here and now. And sometimes that means Gra-Nola baptizes
her niece.

chapter nine | **modesty, manners, and church**

When we moved to Uganda in 1994, we began to learn how differently modesty was defined in another culture. Covering the upper body was not as important as it is in America, and women nursed their babies quite openly in public settings. We came to learn that for Ugandans in rural villages, the primary modesty issue was the lower part of the body: hips, legs, even ankles. So wearing shorts or jeans was immodest and even had sexual and moral implications. Ugandans are more modest than Americans, but they define modesty differently.

If my Ugandan friends could tell you how they perceived me and my American friends, they might tell you that they experienced awkward moments around us. While I appropriately wore dresses and long skirts outside my home, I wore pants and sometimes even shorts in my own house, especially on hot equatorial days when I would grab a wrap-around skirt quickly if someone came for a visit. On one particular day, my friend Robinah surprised me with a visit, and our son Nate escorted her into the house before I had a chance to make myself presentable. When Robinah saw me in my modest baggy shorts, she literally caught her breath, not sure how to react. She couldn't believe I would walk around that way in broad daylight. We later had a good laugh about it, but it was a nervous kind of laugh on her part.

While we were advised early on that women who wear pants or jeans are loose women and likely to be prostitutes, we noticed that appeared to hold true in the rural villages but not in Jinja, the larger town where we lived, or in the capital city, Kampala. In the cities, we saw women who were upstanding citizens wearing pants every day.

While we made some cultural missteps in those early years, we eventually learned the rules of modesty in Uganda, and we watched as those rules morphed through the years, for better or worse, as Western influence became more prevalent through imported magazines, movies, and eventually the Internet.

John tells about one specific experience when changing attitudes about modesty affected a local church. He arrived for a weekly Bible study at the Bunaibamba Church of Christ, and he could hear the church women engaged in heated discussion. They were noticeably upset about something. John began to pick up that they were complaining about another woman in the village, what she does, how she acts. That's not terribly unusual in Uganda or in America. People gossip sometimes, but John was intrigued, so he asked Kawanguzi, his host and one of the church leaders, "Why are all the women so upset?"

Kawanguzi explained that a young woman had come to the village from Kampala for an extended visit. The young woman was wearing jeans and makeup, not just around the village but also when she came to church. While this was common and acceptable in Kampala, it was wildly inappropriate in Bunaibamba in those days. The women were upset and angry, calling her ungodly and accusing her of tempting their husbands. Kawanguzi said that the situation had disrupted the church service on

Sunday. The women were not paying attention to the lesson, some people left frustrated, and other village people came out of curiosity just to see what would happen. Imagine the reactions that would develop if a woman wore a bikini to your church next week!

It was clear to John that the weekly Bible study he had come to lead would be dominated by discussion of the woman's jeans, even though she wasn't present at the study herself. Kawanguzi's wife, Bess, is a strong character. Once when I was leading a Bible study at her house, she was in labor with one of their children, but she participated in the study through her labor pains and gave birth less than an hour after the study concluded. Bess is not one to back away from a challenge. When the group gathered for study, Bess bluntly said that the woman wearing jeans must be brought under control.

At that point, Kawanguzi asked John for help; he suggested that John come back the following week with a study that would help them decide what to do. That calmed things down a bit, and everyone agreed to the plan. John left Bunaibamba that day planning what to do the following week. He planned to emphasize unity, discuss cultural dilemmas with the church, tell disarming stories from American church culture, and cite pertinent instances of cultural decisions in Scripture.

In the meantime, John wrote a letter to the church that read something like this:

> To the Church of Christ in Bunaibamba,
>
> I am encouraged by your faith as a young church. You are growing together, and God is blessing you. I understand that there are some confusions among you regarding modesty and that these confusions are even causing disunity. It's clear that gatherings for study and worship are becoming unmanageable. Even the community around the church

is hearing about the disunity, and this is not good for our Christian witness. I know this is a disputed issue in all our village churches; and therefore, let me ask that women wear modest skirts. None of the women should wear pants to the church meetings until we have a chance to discuss it together.

As Uganda changed during the years we were there, the dynamics of culture and context swirled in more and more churches. Old traditions were left behind, and new traditions emerged. Village church members got cell phones that connected them to a wider world and bought televisions (powered by car batteries where there was no electricity) that brought in shows such as reruns of *Dallas*. I remember convincing a friend that not all women in America dress and act like the women on *Baywatch*. Culture was in a unique time of flux and motion, especially regarding what is modest and decent, and church unity decisions were made in the midst of this chaos. If a woman were to wear jeans to a church service in rural Uganda today, the situation would be significantly different than it was almost twenty years ago, but that's how John handled it at the time.

For the record, John is not opposed to women wearing jeans to church gatherings. His wife and daughter wear jeans in church settings on a regular basis. It does not mean he is constantly changing his mind about important church matters. It does mean that he was contributing to a church unity discussion in a contentious situation and trying to find a way to hold on until unity could be addressed. As a young church looked to him for guidance, he wrote a letter that said women shouldn't wear jeans to church.

By his own account, John was a young, green missionary trying to figure out the complexities of culture and the roles that he should take in a new church. While there are obvious differences between John and Paul,

I still think the example is appropriate as we discuss Paul's interactions with the church in Corinth.

What if, for example, someone got that letter concerning a particular situation between an American church planter and a young church plant in the mid 1990s? What if they took the letter, translated it into languages all over the world, and represented it as if John thinks women should never wear jeans to church? We would see that as ridiculous.

But we do that to Paul sometimes!

There was a time when I read Paul's words, "Women should be silent in the church" as a commandment for all churches in all times and situations. 1 Corinthians 14:33–40 reads as follows:

> For God is not a God of disorder but of peace. As in all the congregations of the Lord's people, women should remain silent in the churches. They are not allowed to speak, but must be in submission, as the Law says. If they want to inquire about something, they should ask their own husbands at home; for it is disgraceful for a woman to speak in the church. Did the word of God originate with you? Or are you the only people it has reached? If anybody thinks he is a prophet or spiritually gifted, let him acknowledge that what I am writing to you is the Lord's command. If he ignores this, he himself will be ignored. Therefore, my brothers, be eager to prophesy, and do not forbid speaking in tongues. But everything should be done in a fitting and orderly way.

It is understandable why this text is used to limit the roles of women in church settings. "Women should remain silent in the churches" is a straightforward command, and Paul even seems to discuss all the congregations of the Lord's people, which could be read as a universal statement for all times. But a consistent universal and literal reading would suggest a gag order of silence. No singing? No questions in Bible class? No shushing of children?

I cannot hope to address every reading of this text in one chapter or even a whole book, but what I can hope to do is explain readings of the passage that first influenced a change in my thought process, from a definitive command for all times and places to a conviction that instead, the text is situational. There's a principle behind what Paul is saying that is universal, but I don't believe the command itself is universal. A church discussion in Uganda in the twentieth century is not the same as one in a first-century church or even one in an American church in the twenty-first century, so stay with me as I explain a reading that makes some sense to me.

I think it helps us understand the situation in Corinth better when we remember the combustible situation as people from all backgrounds and walks of life came together for worship. Paul was addressing issues of worship orderliness in Corinth, and he focused on several cases of disorder, including abuse at the Lord's Supper and the gift of speaking in tongues. It's clear that conflict arose in Corinth about how a diverse group should eat together; social status dictated who shared meals in society. Apparently, the poor in the Corinthian church were going hungry, while the rich were feasting together, all on the pretext of the Lord's Supper (1 Cor. 11). This created great ire within Paul, who preached a gospel that breaks down social barriers. We also see that some church members were exercising gifts of prophecy and tongue speaking in a way that Paul needed to address. This issue related to the diversity of the congregation as well. Some members who came out of cultish religions popular in Corinth would be drawn to ecstatic experiences like tongue speaking, while others, like Paul, came from a word-centered tradition and would be drawn to prophecy. Paul (gifted in tongue speaking himself) didn't teach against all use of tongue speaking, but he did teach that it must not create chaos in worship. Carroll Osburn, in her book *Women in the Church*, points out that Paul also commanded silence in certain situations for some who were creating pandemonium in worship, those speaking in tongues and prophesying without proper orderliness. The word for silence does not occur only in relation to women in the congregation. Paul was dealing with a diversity of issues related to orderly worship (14:26–33).

A significant result of the changing cultural diversity in the Corinthian church was that some women were apparently dominating worship services with uninformed questions and comments. As Paul wrote to the diverse group in Corinth, he needed to address the way women's behavior was contributing to chaos in worship. This dynamic and Paul's advice deserve some focused attention.

There's so much we don't know about what was going on in Corinth regarding gender roles in society because of the diversity of the melting pot culture. There is evidence that some women were active and empowered outside the home, serving as priestesses in cults or active in the business world of Corinth, while others lived in more conservative segments of society in which their lives were almost exclusively in the home.

One aspect of Corinthian life I find intriguing that contributes to the discussion of gender roles in the Corinthian church is the education of women. In their book about the place of women in the house churches of early Christianity, Carolyn Oseik, Margaret MacDonald, and Janet Tulloch discuss cultural evidence which suggests that women from all segments of Corinthian society were less educated than their male counterparts. They write that while it's true that girls in Greco-Roman society sometimes joined boys in rhetorical education outside the home (with the accompaniment of a male chaperone), it was not common beyond grammar school. Even when a relatively liberated woman was singled out for intellectual achievement, she was excluded from the higher forms of rhetorical education associated with public and professional life. In those instances, she received her education at home through a tutor. For most women, education focused primarily on domestic life: spinning, weaving, running a household, and character formation. This education took place in the home, among women who passed on their wisdom to younger women. Despite the evidence of some formally educated women, it was clear that most women were expected primarily to function in the household.

That's a rudimentary explanation of education for Gentile women in the wider Greco-Roman world, and I realize I'm dealing with generalizations that could be more fully explored, but it helps us understand a bit about the background of congregants who received Paul's advice. On another level of understanding, we should note that women in Judaism received even less education than Gentile women in the wider Greco-Roman world. To one extreme, a second-century rabbi, for example, wanted women to learn only enough of the Torah to understand the procedure to be followed if they were suspected of adultery. Those with a more progressive view, however, allowed women to attend rabbinical schools, but very few rabbinical schools included women disciples (although Jesus seems to have allowed them: Mark 15:40–41; Luke 8:1–3, 10:38–42).

The main point here is that Christian women from Jewish backgrounds were not likely to receive a formal education. Even many liberated Corinthian women, while perhaps more educated than their Jewish sisters, weren't educated alongside male church members with whom they worshiped, ate, and learned in the church community.

Craig Keener, in his book *Paul, Women, and Wives*, indicates that a central skill those male church members learned in their educational experience was the art of asking appropriate questions. Greco-Roman education, the pervasive approach to education in first-century Corinth, insisted that a student was rude if he jumped into a discussion before he knew what he was talking about, so he must learn to ask informed questions. Interrupting a lecture with ignorant comments or even whispering during a lecture was highly disrespectful. I imagine that Plutarch, a first-century historian and educator, would not have appreciated the texting or Facebook posting that takes place in classrooms today. Consider his words about a proper learning environment:

> But those who instantly interrupt with contradictions, neither hearing nor being heard, but talking while others talk, behave in an unseemly manner; whereas the man who has the habit of listening with restraint and respect, takes in and masters a useful discourse, and more readily sees through and detects a useless or a false one, showing himself thus to be a lover of truth and not a lover of disputation, nor forward and contentious.

Plutarch and countless other sources regarding Greco-Roman educational theory emphasized that a quiet demeanor was the appropriate demeanor for learning until a student had a thorough knowledge of the subject. Some teachers even required long periods of contemplative silence from their students as a way of teaching them to be disciplined thinkers. Men were cultivated to express a quiet demeanor and appropriate forms of engagement in learning, while women were educated in the kitchen, where it wasn't likely they raised their hands before asking questions.

When we take all these factors into consideration—conservative Judaism, new Gentile Christians, educational backgrounds, gender roles—we must realize that when the church came together for worship in Corinth, it's an understatement to say that the membership was diverse. The church was in a time of ongoing change and adaptation.

It's beautiful to realize that early Christianity made a place for women, slaves, Gentiles, and Jews even though their secular world was built on gender, class, ethnic, and educational distinctions. It was radical. The diverse early church was nonetheless a beautiful picture of unity in the model of the trinity of Father, Son, and Holy Spirit.

Picture, however, how the beautiful picture was compromised when some church members disrupted gatherings with bad manners, inappropriate conversation, ill-timed questions, and perceived immodesty. It's not hard to imagine that a problem specific to women rose in the Corinthian church. In light of their new liberty and their place at the table, is it possible that some women were being disruptive with their questions and comments in a way that wasn't appropriate for a communal environment? Perhaps they weren't making the adjustment from their household learning style to the learning style of a larger group of people. For the sake of order, Paul told them to exercise quiet restraint. According to Keener, when women were given new freedom in church, their lack of education became an issue as they tried to participate publicly. Simply put, they were talking about things they didn't really know enough to talk about, and it became disruptive for the group.

The picture was no longer beautiful or a reflection of the Holy Trinity. The church was challenged in its unity as a result of the cultural diversity and ongoing change in Corinth. I can imagine conversations that took place before and after church meetings in which some women complained that others were piping up too much. Or perhaps men were complaining that women were asking uneducated questions. It could be that some women were demanding that they should be able to teach and prophesy, even though they did not have the gift or education for those roles. I can see that Paul, a missionary at heart, would look at the disunity and see that it was offensive to the very culture the church should be evangelizing. The primary principle was that the gospel must be proclaimed, and that unity must become part of the witness to a surrounding culture of God's presence, thus proclamation.

There, I think, we have insight regarding the situation that led to Paul's injunction in 1 Corinthians 14:34, "Women should remain silent in the churches."

Paul was careful with his words in his advice to Corinth. He was speaking to a situation in which men were given an education and intellectual dominance, and most women were not. Many husbands would not think their wives capable of taking part in communal discussion appropriately. In his response, Paul advocated a progressive view that would move toward inclusion. Paul told the husbands to see the potential in their wives. He told them to recognize the women's intellectual capacities and to begin the process of tending to their education at home so that they would know the right questions to ask and how to ask them when they came together in worship. The husbands were to teach their wives that learning in silence and with a submissive demeanor was as valued for women as it was for men.

Both Keener and Osburn point out that in his well-known command, Paul gave a long-range solution to the inappropriate, situation-specific questions among the uninformed women in Corinth. We must open our minds to the moving cultural situation in Corinth so that we can grasp how culturally progressive Paul's idea was. Permitting and even encouraging women to learn how to ask questions was a radical suggestion for some members of the church. Paul gave similar advice in 1 Timothy 2 when he advised women to learn in quiet and full submission, another context where newfound liberty was creating communal challenges.

Paul's advice in 1 Corinthians 14 was not a *permanent* solution for *all* women for *all* times. He was not mapping out the next two thousand years of Christian gender relations in one sentence. Paul was addressing problems that were disrupting the church as new freedom was given and sometimes abused in this specific Corinthian setting.

Paul was taking care that the church should not create a shameful spectacle of disorderly worship that would drive seekers away from hearing the gospel.

In Western churches today, male and female members have all experienced proper educational etiquette (texting and Facebook aside), and we are faced with a different situation and a different challenge in our churches.

Our wider society, for the most part, recognizes that men and women serve well alongside one another in their unique God-given glory, one neither better than the other nor exactly the same, but each with gifts to bring to the table. Unfortunately, in great extent due to our misunderstanding of 1 Corinthians 14:34, many of our churches have not placed our chairs around an inclusive table. We're missing the great fellowship that comes when God's image is most exquisitely displayed in community and diversity with one another. We're missing the outcome of the grand story of God in which all are made one in Christ, the story Paul hoped the Corinthian church would embrace when they gathered for fellowship in a kingdom where power and status are defined by the body and blood of Christ.

Let me pose some questions that I have pondered as I consider the situation in Corinth: If Paul walked into one of our churches today, where we are in an entirely different cultural setting in which women in our pews are superintendents of our schools, prosecuting attorneys in our courtrooms, clinical psychologists, presidents of our banks, and professors in our universities, is it conceivable that Paul might say exactly the opposite of what he said in Corinth? Could he say to our congregations that it's scandalous that women can't hand out bulletins, serve communion, pray, and preach? Is it possible that Paul might tell us that we are out of step with culture and that we're creating a shameful spectacle that will drive people away from participation in the gospel?

If Paul said to women in Corinth that they were culturally overstepping their bounds and becoming obstacles to the gospel, is it imaginable that he would say the opposite to us now because of the same principle?

Paul was applying a principle in Corinth that would advance the gospel, but that principle might look different in another situation. How we follow the principle in order to advance the gospel might look different in Rochester, Michigan, or Jinja, Uganda, or Searcy, Arkansas. It might even be the opposite of what Paul advocated in Corinth.

As I wrote earlier in this chapter, I am presenting one reading of a highly disputed text. There are a vast number of others. What should happen if I share this interpretation of Scripture in my Sunday school class next Sunday morning and others in the class disagree with me? What if one of my brothers or sisters in Christ says, "Sara, that's just not what I've always been taught. It's clear—women are to be silent in the church. Silence for women means that they should not preach or teach or even speak at all in worship. My interpretation does not have room for distinctions between learning and teaching and cultural changes." Is it possible for the two of us to experience *common unity* despite our differences in interpretation? How do we decide which of us should compromise?

At some point in my journey with the quagmire of interpretations surrounding gender roles, I remember flipping back and forth between two of our integral texts about women in 1 Corinthians. There was a period when I wore out my Bible between those texts. I wondered why Paul said, "women may pray and prophesy" in one instance (1 Cor. 11) and then told them to "be silent" in another (1 Cor. 14). I questioned, "What were you thinking, Paul?" I even prayed aloud, "God, help me." Somewhere between those texts, as I flipped back and forth, God mysteriously reached out and grabbed my attention. Nestled between those texts and giving definition to both are striking words God used to answer my prayer.

> If I speak in the tongues of men and of angels, but have not
> love, I am only a resounding gong or a clanging cymbal. If I

have the gift of prophecy and can fathom all mysteries and all knowledge, and if I have a faith that can move mountains, but have not love, I am nothing. If I give all I possess to the poor and surrender my body to the flames, but have not love, I gain nothing.

[I might add, "If I understand correctly all nuances of the discussion of gender roles in church, but have not love, I am nothing."]

Love is patient, love is kind. It does not envy, it does not boast, it is not proud. It is not rude, it is not self-seeking, it is not easily angered, it keeps no record of wrongs. Love does not delight in evil but rejoices with the truth. It always protects, always trusts, always hopes, always perseveres. Love never fails. (1 Cor. 13:1–8a)

These words may sound naïve as we face this explosive issue in our churches. These words may not provide the textual proof that some would like to "solve" the gender issue. But these words more than any other have guided me and chastised me and given me hope. It's my opinion that we cannot settle this merely by appealing to specific texts. That's where my interpretative process differs from some others. I'm convinced that how we read Scripture is just as important as what we read. I prefer not to look at isolated texts but at broad theological themes and redemptive movement throughout the big story of Scripture. The texts that have guided me most along this journey are those of love and unity, like 1 Corinthians 13.

If these words were important to the Corinthian Christians as Paul wrote to them about how to conduct church properly and in order, then they are important for all of us as we do the same. It's with people like those Paul describes as patient, kind, not envious, not boastful, and not proud that we have hope of common unity.

I personalized the passage in my journal that day as I wrote a version of 1 Corinthians 13 applied to my own church setting (long before Rob Bell's book *Love Wins*).

> Sara, as you find yourself caught in the middle of this gender worship war, remember that love wins. If you think you have the gift of understanding all the controversial texts related to the gender issue, but you do not have love, you are nothing. If you can fathom the full mystery of this issue, and if you have all knowledge of the Greek language and the cultural context of antiquity, but you do not have love, you gain nothing.
>
> Sara, love never fails. It does not envy men who are affirmed for their gifts of teaching. It does not envy women who are fulfilled in their traditional gifts. It does not dishonor others who read those texts differently. It is not easily given to self-righteous anger. It does not keep a record of wrongs perpetrated against women in churches. Love trusts other people and hopes in their goodness and perseveres to bring truth and light into every situation.
>
> Sara, love will not fail you. New creation is happening all around you. What you are experiencing now is only a reflection in a mirror. Something more is coming. One day you will fully know and fully be known. For now Sara, remember, love wins.

Some will find such a conclusion naïve, idealistic, impractical, or even foolish. Honestly, sometimes I do, too. I do not always want to trust God in this, but I choose to. And in Christ, love wins. Through the power of the Spirit, love unifies. God helps us love one another, so, God help me—I choose love. And that's my final answer.

But God chose the foolish things of the world to shame the wise; God chose the weak things of the world to shame the strong. God chose the lowly things of this world and the despised things—and the things that are not—to nullify the things that are, so that no one may boast before him. (1 Cor. 1:27–29)

chapter ten | **you are where you sit**

So God created humankind in his own image,
in the image of God he created him;
male and female he created them. (Gen. 1:27 NRSV)

According to Genesis, when humans were created, God walked with them, and they lived in harmony and loving community. Although there are varied interpretations among serious scholars regarding the relationship between Adam and Eve, the interpretations of Genesis 1–3 that resonate most with me are those that emphasize hierarchy among humans as a result of the fall rather than as built in at creation. Some interpret the creation account to say that because Adam was created first, men were created to be higher in rank than women. Others interpret the story to mean that Eve is superior because God saved the best for last. Both interpretations seem to me to be anachronistic.

Let me explain "anachronistic." That's when something is included in an artistic piece that didn't exist in the time period being referenced. A well-known example is found in Shakespeare's *Julius Caesar* (act II, scene i, lines 202–204):

> Brutus: Peace! Count the clock.
>
> Cassius: The clock has stricken three.

There were no clocks during Roman times, and the striking clock was not invented until fourteen hundred years after Caesar's death. Shakespeare referred to something that didn't exist during the time he was portraying. That's an anachronism.

The movie *Forrest Gump* is a favorite for finding anachronisms. For example, Forrest receives a letter from Apple Computer dated September 21, 1975, when Apple wasn't founded until January 3, 1977.

We can also find anachronisms in classic art. Sixteenth-century Italian painter Caravaggio often used them in his interpretations of biblical scenes. A well-known example is his *Sacrifice of Isaac*. Caravaggio used great care in depicting a look of terror on Isaac's face as his father held a knife over him. As we tear our gaze from Isaac's face and look deeper into the painting, we see that Caravaggio has set the scene not in the wilderness of Mount Moriah but in a pleasant Roman landscape. Caravaggio's use of anachronism is positive in this sense. By bringing Abraham and Isaac to Rome, he poignantly forces viewers of his work to remember that the scene is not simply a detached, ancient story but ongoing and open ended. Caravaggio's work invites us into Genesis 22, reminding us that this is our story and that we are a part of the drama even in our day and age. We cannot look at that painting without wondering what we would have done in Abraham's time and place or considering how the action challenges us in our own time and place.

Anachronism sometimes is inadvertent, but sometimes it is used intentionally for artistic purposes. It is about projecting something from the future into a past time when that thing did not exist, and that's what happens when we go to Genesis before the fall and start looking for hierarchy between Adam and Eve. Reading modern ideas of gender inequality into Genesis is anachronistic. Modern definitions of equality in a democratic society of citizenship and equal opportunity employment should not be superimposed onto Genesis 1 and 2 to prove what our society deems to be politically correct. Alternately, it's also anachronistic to go there to determine who is in charge, who is superior, or who is dominant. Those interpretive approaches involve putting our broken definition of power into Genesis 1 and 2. That's anachronistic. Instead, let's seek God's definition of power, the kind of power that existed before the fall.

Power is certainly a significant theme in Genesis 1–3. My colleague, Craig Bowman, shared a lecture of his with me that rightly celebrates power in creation. As king, God commands order to come out of chaos. With unparalleled power, God arranges all aspects of the order created as the only one capable of doing so. And in that order, human beings are created in God's image and likeness. In Genesis 1:26, God says that humans will have dominion over all of creation. As representatives of God, human beings, both male and female, rule over the earth and its creatures. They are emissaries for the king. Being made in the image of God empowers both male and female to represent God as they exercise authority over all other creatures entrusted to their care or dominion. When the world is constructed, humans are to carry out God's work as stewards in and for the world, with high moral and vocational expectations. God does not say, however, that humans rule over each other. That power belongs only to God as the Creator King whose sovereignty is not to be rivaled.

The change in relationship between male and female comes as the narrative of Genesis 1–3 unfolds. As king, it is God who grants humans power over certain realms. In chapter one, when creation is whole, this power is a blessing to be used responsibly. In chapter three, after creation is spoiled, the power a husband has over his wife is a curse, the result of rebellion in the garden. Both blessing and curse come from God, who holds humans accountable for how they use and abuse their divinely bestowed power.

When we discuss relationships between male and female, it's important for us to remember that Adam and Eve were originally created for a relationship in which power was not distorted in the way we define it in our broken world. It was when sin entered the world that relationships between male and female were broken. It was then that distorted power started to exert power over us. Carroll Osburn writes about power and Eden:

> The essence of the first sin in Eden is the desire for independent power (Gen. 3:5). Nothing suggests that they violated some so-called "divine order of male dominance"—rather, their sin was disobedience and wanting to be like God (3:5–7, 11). The desire for dominance over others is the root of much moral evil—war, slavery, murder, theft, cruelty, etc. "He shall rule over you" (Gen. 3:16) comes as a result of the fall and was not part of God's original intention.

The temptation for both Adam and Eve (and for the Adams and Eves to follow) was to give up the harmonious relationship with God in their proper place as God's subjects and be independent. I am aware of alternative interpretations, but in Genesis 1 and 2, I believe they shared a hierarchy-free relationship in which power had its right place, a power based on humility rather than pride. The fall shattered that harmony and began the battle of the sexes; patriarchy is a result of the fall, not something God originally designed for humanity.

In Genesis, God told Adam and Eve what would happen as a result of what was shattered. In essence, God declared to them how history would work because of what they had done. Adam and Eve were told that the heartache they introduced would create competition between them, and that they would look out for themselves more than for the other. God told them they would suffer from what they initiated, and it's clear that creation would suffer under their dominion as well.

I don't think it's necessarily punishment God was prescribing in the curse. The only things cursed are the serpent and the ground. God was telling the first humans bluntly what they had brought on themselves. In the basic social relationship that was meant to be harmonious and communal on God's behalf, distorted power and a desire for selfish dominance infiltrated human existence, and this pride-filled power began to grow.

Trying to find hierarchy and dominance between humans before the fall is like Julius Caesar pulling the tab off his Dr Pepper before logging on to his Apple computer on Mount Moriah.

But that's not the end of the story. Our Bibles contain more than the first three chapters. With Adam and Eve's departure from Eden, God initiated the creation of something new. In a great act of grace, God didn't leave them in Eden to suffer hopelessly but made the first move of redemption in which shattered creation, tainted with pride-filled power and dominance, would be renewed. Scot McKnight puts it like this in *The Blue Parakeet*: "The redemptive plan of the Bible is to restore humans into a oneness relationship with God, self, others, and the world."

Scripture does not teach that God's kind of renewal is a snap of the finger. It's not a genie-in-a-bottle, make-a-wish kind of renewal.

God's partnership with humans for renewed creation gives us clues for what power is supposed to look like, what it was like before the fall, when it was very good. When God most clearly revealed what human relationships should be, it was in a person, Jesus of Nazareth. It's through that person that humanity is invited to join a community that embodies God's definition of humble power. Paul says that the kingdom of God is not talk, but power (1 Cor. 4:20). Kingdom power is understood through humility to be very good. Humility produces fruit that pride does not. Because pride has no real power, it must resort to violence to maintain its place. Christians, however, live according to power as revealed through Jesus, and that changes everything.

Through a covenant with Israel, God joined with humanity in a story that culminated with a redefinition of relational power in this world of hierarchy. It climaxed when God's own son was born as a human baby, lived a life that resisted the temptation of worldly power and independence, suffered on a cross at the hands of the very power-hungry humans who disobeyed his Father, and was resurrected to make known that the death of harmonious community that came at the fall would not claim the final word. Jesus Christ overcame that which divided all God's children (Gal. 3:13).

It's through Jesus that Christians believe distorted human desire for power no longer holds ultimate power over our lives, and it's through Jesus that we glimpse what humility-pervasive power was really meant to be. It's through a servant who humbly emptied himself of power that power is understood. Philippians 2:7 makes it clear that Jesus gave up his divine privileges, poured out his equality with God, and took the humble position of a servant. His example shows us how we should wield power extravagantly as Christ followers.

Through Jesus, and through the power of the Holy Spirit in our lives, Christian believers have the opportunity to join what God is doing to heal what was broken. God worked through covenant with Israel and through the Law to bring about the opportunity for all to be heirs through faith. This makes me think of what Paul says in Galatians 3:

> But Scripture has locked up everything under the control of
> sin, so that what was promised, being given through faith

in Jesus Christ, might be given to those who believe. Before the coming of this faith, we were held in custody under the law, locked up until the faith that was to come would be revealed. So the law was our guardian until Christ came that we might be justified by faith. Now that this faith has come, we are no longer under a guardian. So in Christ Jesus you are all children of God through faith, for all of you who were baptized into Christ have clothed yourselves with Christ. There is neither Jew nor Gentile, neither slave nor free, nor is there male and female, for you are all one in Christ Jesus. If you belong to Christ, then you are Abraham's seed, and heirs according to the promise. (Gal. 3:22–29)

The promise has been fulfilled, and we're no longer held in custody. What was initiated because of Adam and Eve's disobedience is reversed. Christ has come, and all the Father's heirs are invited to the table.

A few years ago, I read an interesting business article about power in relationships titled "You Are Where You Sit." The author, Aili McConnon, writes that in the business world, "where you sit influences where you stand." Here's how she explains it:

> The person with the most power determines how everybody else positions themselves around the typical rectangular or oblong office table. As a rule, leaders like to sit at the end of the table facing the exit so no one can sneak up on them.

The article caught my attention because it utilized *Snow White and the Seven Dwarfs* as a means of understanding these seating arrangements. I learned that Grumpy personality types usually sit across from the leader; they are vocal and even argumentative. Happy types, however, tend to sit on the leader's right and use flattery as a means of securing a place of influence. Apparently, wise managers take these personality types into consideration and arrange seating in order to improve their chances of influencing the discussion toward their goals and as a means of empowering or disempowering their allies and foes.

This article demonstrates that the shattered world understands power at the table through hierarchical definitions. Power is currency around those tables.

Those who follow Jesus, however, define "you are where you sit" differently than the world when we gather around the table. Jesus began not by seeking to establish control through psychological power games but by humbling himself. He washed the feet of his disciples, and later when he "could have called ten thousand angels to destroy the world and set him free," he resisted the temptation for worldly power. Jesus did not consider his inherent equality with God something to be used to his own advantage. Instead, he made himself nothing by taking the very nature of a servant. Jesus humbled himself, even to death on a cross (Phil. 2:5–8).

When we define power through the example of Jesus, we see a suffering servant, one who serves creation. At least part of what believers must do is to continually redefine power as God most clearly revealed it to us through Jesus.

Let's stop asking who gets to do what in church at 10 A.M. on Sunday morning.

That's the wrong question.

Let's start asking how we can avoid falling prey to a shattered world's definition of power.

part four | **together**

chapter eleven | **whippoorwills and worship**

In 1990, I was dating a guy I really liked, a guy I was quite sure I loved, actually. It was the first time he was going to meet my family in my little hometown, Melbourne, Arkansas, and I was nervous. All my siblings had married spouses from our hometown, but this guy was not from my hometown (from a galaxy far, far away in Philadelphia, Pennsylvania). This guy knew nothing about Melbourne and my world, and I was nervous, as people usually are under those circumstances. I wondered how much deer meat John would be offered to eat (it turned out he loved it) and how much he would need to know about the only sports team that counted, the Arkansas Razorbacks. There was, however, one part of taking John Barton home with me that I was *not* nervous about.

There's this lookout point (okay, call it a *makeout* point if you want) on Highway 9, just outside of Melbourne. Highway 9 is the curviest and most windy road I've ever experienced. It follows an old pioneer wagon trail. There's one stretch of the road that winds around and around like several letter Ss all strung together, seemingly just for the fun of it. My dad explained to me that there used to be trees in the crooks of the Ss.

The trees have long since died or been chopped down, but the road still curves around as if the trees were still obstructing the path of horses and wagons. It's a carsick-for-sure kind of road.

The drive is worth getting carsick, though, because it's beautiful country. The foothills of the Ozark Mountains are gorgeous. No electric poles, no houses, no smoky chimneys. Just plain old beauty. Since I left that little Arkansas town, I've skied in the Rocky Mountains, hiked in the Alps, spied a leopard in the shadow of Kilimanjaro, and tracked gorillas in the Rwenzori Mountains of Uganda. Even after seeing all those exotic places, I still think our little Highway 9 drive from Melbourne to Mountain View is one of the prettiest places on God's earth.

That's where I wanted to take John. I had it all planned out—timed at sunset with a blanket and hot chocolate. We were holding hands, back when holding hands made my heart beat in rhythm with the lightning bugs all around us in the early evening sky.

When we arrived and got settled, I thought our date was turning out just as I had planned. Romance. Kisses. A gentle evening breeze. A bird's call in the distance, a whippoorwill, added the final touch that I couldn't have planned. I've never actually *seen* a whippoorwill, probably because they are nocturnal creatures, but I've heard their call my whole life. They call repetitively, as part of their courtship, in a sound like the name of the bird. It's onomatopoetic. The name of the bird comes from the sound it makes. "Whip-poor-will." The whippoorwill female may alight near a calling male, who then walks toward her, circling and bobbing as both birds call continuously. Or he may approach her from alternating sides, touching her bill as she trembles. You never thought a bird could be rated PG-13, did you?

To give you an even clearer impression of my country-perfect date, I should tell you that country singer Randy Travis was my favorite musician at that time. Randy Travis sings a song called "Deeper than the Holler," and the chorus of the song described our little adventure that evening:

My love is deeper than the holler, stronger than the river
Higher than the pine trees growin' tall up on the hill
My love is purer than the snowflakes that fall in late December
And honest as a robin on a springtime windowsill
And longer than the call of a whippoorwill.

We sat and talked a while as Randy Travis's ballad played in my mind. I was in this dream world where everything was peaceful and beautiful and romantic for us lovebirds, until my dream was shattered with a bombshell from John: "I need to get out of here. That stupid bird is driving me crazy."

City boys from Philadelphia, it turns out, do not appreciate whippoorwills the way country girls from the hollers of Arkansas do.

I tell this story because that was one of those times when it was clear that two people can experience the same event in dramatically different ways, depending on what they are accustomed to. Personalities. Backgrounds. Experiences. Likes. Dislikes. They all swirl around inside us and cause us to be complicated, unique individuals who can experience the same moment in time very differently. One little detail, like a whippoorwill's call, can make an immense difference to us.

A similar situation happens sometimes when it comes to worship.

Two people sit in the same auditorium and hear the same songs and spoken words, but something happens in the details and brings about dramatically different reactions. One person leaves a time of worship fulfilled, uplifted, and close to God. Someone else leaves the same worship experience frustrated, distant from God, and disconnected from others. What causes the connect and the disconnect often comes down to differences in perception of the worship. A certain song may touch one worshiper who remembers that the song was sung on the night of her baptism, and she feels uplifted. Another worshiper hears the same song and is irritated by how the words are awkwardly placed in order to bring about a rhyme, and disconnect takes place. Same song. Different experiences.

Sometimes contradictory reactions to the same worship service are the result of generational traditions and experiences. When John and I were young newlyweds and were ministering to a small congregation in Brownsville, Tennessee, we learned significant lessons about how the older Christian members there defined respectful worship as compared to our generation. A stated goal of this congregation was to give young seminary students like John a chance to preach in an environment where the members would give the student (and his wife) significant feedback about how to work with a church. It was something John and I both needed to learn, and they were the perfect group to teach us. They loved us, fed us lunch every Sunday, prayed for us, and corrected us gently. When our son Nate was born, they were among the first friends to show up at the hospital; when we moved to Uganda, they were the first friends to send a care package. Every young preacher should have a church like the New Hope Church of Christ.

Many of the lessons we learned about generational worship perspectives came from Panny Baldy (her real name). The experience of Panny Baldy defies description. She was kind, opinionated, feisty, talkative, thoughtful, devoted, Southern-to-the-core . . . words fail to capture Panny's essence. She once told us the story of how she auditioned and came in second to play the role of Granny in the old television show *The Beverly Hillbillies.*

Panny taught me a lesson about her perception of worship in a conversation that has stuck with me through the years. She told me she had heard that in one of the big churches in Memphis, people were taking their morning coffee into the auditorium. This was 1992, well before the Starbucks boom and the acceptability of coffee shops in church lobbies. Panny said that worshipers should give their best to God on Sunday mornings, not look lazy, crumpled, and relaxed with a cup of coffee. Furthermore, Panny told me that if worshipers took coffee into the sanctuary, they would be tempted to take a sip of coffee between the passing of the bread and the fruit of the vine, which was, to her, a blatant sign of disrespectful worship, and for Panny, taking the Lord's Supper incorrectly was, in her words, "a salvation issue."

When I take my coffee to church these days, I often think about Panny Baldy, and I'm careful to keep my coffee drinking and my participation in communion separate from each other, sometimes with a little chuckle about how times have changed. The point of the story is that what is considered respectful and correct changes from one generation to the next. Young folks just don't define respectful worship the same way their grandparents did. They experience the whippoorwill aspects of worship differently, and lines are often drawn between what affects salvation and what does not.

Each worshiper brings a unique perspective to communal worship. Sometimes it's generational, but all kinds of background differences can become factors. Sometimes what we bring to worship is wrapped up in our beliefs and doctrines and what we've always been taught. However, what one person has always been taught is not the same as what another person has always been taught. What one person considers traditional worship is not another's tradition. What one considers disrespectful, another finds to be respectful. A beautiful moment in worship (like a beautiful whippoorwill call) brings a moment of dissonance for someone else.

My whippoorwill analogy works up to a certain point. John reacted to the whippoorwill differently than I did because he hadn't been exposed to one before. I had spent my life sleeping in whippoorwill country, with the warm summer breeze bringing the bird's call into my bedroom in a comforting kind of way. I had heard stories from my dad about how the strange birds got quiet when his hunting dogs barked on his raccoon-hunting expeditions in the dark night. I had sung quaint country music songs and thought of whippoorwills in a romantic context. John was not accustomed to the repetitive, monotonous, unending, shrill noise.

When I talk about discomfort in communal worship as the "whippoorwill factor," I am saying that some of the discomfort during worship is mainly due to a lack of exposure to those worship practices, not that there is anything *wrong* with the practice.

Some Christians refer to certain aspects of worship as "salvation issues" and discuss whether worship practices affect the salvation of souls. It's not just about preferences, likes, or dislikes. For many Christians, the very mechanics of worship are connected to fear of God's wrath. Many Christians have been taught that if they worship in a way that is not pleasing to God and in alignment with God's Word, their mistakes could lead to a change in the status of their salvation. Some consider the participation of women in communal worship to be one of those salvation issues, believing that if women teach, preach, or pray, those present in the assembly endanger their souls.

To many serious worshipers, the participation of women in worship is not merely an irritant, and it's not merely something to which they have not been exposed. It's not something to be compared to a silly bird because it is clearly forbidden by God. That's where the analogy comes to a halt in the minds of many. For them, Scripture clearly forbids women to speak in worship, taking the issue far beyond comfort or familiarity and considering it an issue connected to salvation.

As is clear through my story, I do not view the participation of women in worship as a practice that inherently influences the salvation of an individual or those participating in communal worship. That discussion is important to me. Arguments that matter to people like Panny Baldy matter to me, because people matter to me.

Worship is important to Christians. It should be. What happens is that sometimes the way we worship can become as much a part of our Christian identity as whom we worship. We can begin to idolize our worship more than we worship God. It's good that we are passionate about our worship, but the downside of that intensity is that we have a tendency to get so worried about that one hour of Sunday morning worship that we spend a majority of our time thinking and planning for that one hour, and the real work of the church is neglected. When we're more concerned about human comfort and discomfort in worship than we are with joining God in the work of salvation going on all around us every day of the week, something is amiss. It seems to me that's when our worship ceases to serve its divine purpose.

It is important for us to ask ourselves how salvation and worship are connected. Salvation is serious, and worship is serious. But neither salvation nor worship has ever primarily been about what's comfortable when we define comfort from a human perspective. More often, it's about what's uncomfortable. If we seek to emulate the New Testament church as our example, we must define salvation and worship outside our own time and place.

Some aspects of worship are about preferences, traditions, and what's always been taught in our communities. It's important in a community of believers to respect the thoughts of others in our groups, because that's something to which we are called—looking to the interests of others. But we cannot allow ourselves to worship comfort more than we worship God.

I've heard people talk about salvation issues my entire life, but it's time to discuss what we mean when we say that. If by "salvation" we mean that one's status before God is in danger when women participate in church ministries, then I don't believe it rises to a salvation issue. I don't think that if a woman preaches at congregational gatherings next Sunday it's going to change whether or not she or anyone else in the congregation goes to heaven. It's not a salvation issue in that sense.

From my perspective, women's participation in public leadership roles clearly does not put anyone's personal salvation at risk. It doesn't change our status before God concerning eternal life, even though I know that some of my sisters and brothers view it that way.

It's my conviction that salvation is bigger than that. In one way, I want to make this issue less important than some fellow believers do. I believe we should stop saying that participation of women in church ministries is "a salvation issue" that will endanger our salvation.

In other ways, however, I want to make it more important than my fellow believers do. Salvation, as I understand it, is much more than a heaven or hell status. Salvation—being saved—is about participating in a way of life offered to us by God. It means belonging to a community that understands power and community differently than a world that seeks to dominate and exclude other human beings. Hear Paul's words about being saved, noting where I've added emphasis:

> For the message of the cross is foolishness to those who are perishing, but to us who are *being saved* it is the power of God. For it is written: "I will destroy the wisdom of the wise; the intelligence of the intelligent I will frustrate."
>
> . . . Brothers and sisters, think of what you were when you were called. Not many of you were wise by human standards; not many were influential; not many were of noble birth. But God chose the foolish things of the world to shame the wise; God chose the weak things of the world to shame the strong. God chose the lowly things of this world and the despised things—and the things that are not—to nullify the things that are, so that no one may boast before him. It is

because of him that you are in Christ Jesus, who has become
for us wisdom from God—that is, our righteousness, holiness and redemption. Therefore, as it is written: "Let the
one who boasts boast in the Lord." (1 Cor. 1:18–19, 26–31)

If we are being saved as Paul defines it, full participation of women in the
community of God is a salvation issue. It *does* bear on what we mean when
we discuss salvation issues. My favorite story about salvation and worship
is the story of the woman at the well.

In John 4, Jesus spoke to a woman about the kind of worshipers our
Father seeks. We read that Jesus "just had to go through Samaria." I love
to imagine how the disciples spoke that little phrase among themselves
as they went into a town in Samaria to look for food. It must have been
a challenge to find food, for Jews and Samaritans didn't even eat from
the same dishes. Were they looking for a kosher deli in Sychar? Were
they relegated to a light snack of fresh fruit instead of a hot meal so they
could avoid tainted food? Maybe one of them, probably Peter, muttered
as they looked for food, "Why didn't we take the route all good Jews take,
the one around Samaria instead of straight through this God-forsaken
place? There's a really great traveler's inn over in Perea where you can get
a good meal of fresh fish and bread. Going through Samaria—this is just
like Jesus. He can't do anything the easy way. He just *had* to go through
Samaria."

As the disciples looked for food, Jesus waited at Jacob's well, where
he struck up a conversation with a Samaritan woman. She was getting
water for her household, and she was later than the other women who had
already been to the well and returned home to their husbands and children. Maybe the Samaritan woman belatedly came to the well to avoid
all the other women for some reason. Maybe she had no children whose
clothes she would rush to wash or whose food she would cook. Maybe she

had overslept that day and was just feeling lazy. Minding her own business, she was filling her water jar, properly avoiding the lone man at the well as it wasn't polite for a woman to carry on a conversation with a strange man.

In addition to the gender divide that would prevent the woman from a conversation, the text indicates she could identify the man as a Jew, perhaps from his clothing, or maybe it was his accent when he asked her for a drink of water. One thing she knew for sure, Jews hated Samaritans. There was a long-standing feud between the groups because, even though the tribes were technically cousins, the Samaritans had aided the Syrians in wars against Israel and had hindered the restoration of Jerusalem after the Babylonian exile. Jews hated Samaritans for their part in their historical disgrace.

Jesus' simple request for the Samaritan woman to give him a drink of water crossed chasms of division. Political adversaries. Jew and Samaritan. Male and female.

The woman probably looked at Jesus across those chasms and bluntly said what she was thinking. "How could you, a Jew, ask me, a Samaritan woman, for a drink of water, for we don't associate with each other or even use the same dishes?" Throughout the Gospels, however, we see that Jesus was not hindered by relational chasms of his day. Jesus connected with people where they were, and that's what he did in this conversation. As Jesus went all over Galilee and through Samaria in this instance, he modeled the original seeker-sensitive worship. Jesus talked about the obvious topic of conversation at a well: water. But Jesus didn't talk just about water; he talked about *living* water. Even though he initially asked the woman for a drink, he reversed the flow of the conversation and told her that he could give her water that really matters.

The woman saw that this man was speaking with authority on theological matters, so in response to his ice breaker about water, she said in essence, "So, who do you think you are—are you greater than Jacob who gave us this well and its water from which we receive physical life? If you have access to something more than that, you intrigue me because I might not have to keep coming back here with my heavy water jar day after day."

It was then that Jesus proved to the woman that he did have access to something more than water. He told her to go call her husband, and I imagine her eyes dropped to the ground in shame. Jesus told her what he couldn't have known about her, that she'd had five husbands and was living with a sixth man. I've sometimes heard preachers call this woman a sinful woman, and it's true that she was sinful because all human beings are sinful. The idea that she was sinful because of failed marriages, however, might be a misunderstanding. I've often wondered if the reason a woman in ancient Israel would have had several husbands, passed around from one man to another, could be because she was barren, unable to have children. Maybe her husbands and her prospects just got worse and worse as she tried to survive as a barren woman. Getting a job and surviving on her own was not an option in ancient Samaria in the way it is in our culture today.

Whatever this woman's circumstance, Jesus realized that her life had been difficult. Her relationships were broken, and yet something in Jesus' tone showed her that he reached beyond those chasms and saw her as she was created to be. In a short sentence or two, Jesus took the conversation straight to the woman's heart and soul. As he spoke to her, I imagine she was able to lift her downcast, shamed gaze and see the eyes of Jesus who knew everything about her but respected and loved her anyway.

It's amusing to me what the woman did when Jesus saw into her soul that way. We all do it! When things get intimate on a spiritual level, and we just don't want to go there, we often do what she did next: We change the subject to a safer religious activity: doctrinal arguments, worship arguments. Let's admit it; it's much easier to argue about doctrine than it is to let Jesus look into our souls. It's safer to ask questions about who's in and who's out, who's saved and who's not, than it is to really understand what God means by salvation. She says, in effect (and I picture her crossing her arms in a bit of a challenge as she says it), "Sir, I can see you are a prophet, so let's talk doctrine. Should we worship here on this mountain, as we Samaritans argue, or should we worship in Jerusalem, as you Jews argue? Answer that salvation issue for me, won't you?"

Jesus responded to her as I think he responds to us today. In essence, he told her to raise her gaze and look salvation straight in the eyes when he said that the Messiah is from the Jews. When she presented her salvation check list, he pointed at what would happen through himself and said, "[A] time is coming and has now come when the true worshipers will worship the Father in the Spirit and in truth, for they are the kind of worshipers the Father seeks. God is spirit, and his worshipers must worship in the Spirit and in truth" (John 4:23–24).

We can argue about what's comfortable or uncomfortable in worship—we can argue about what's a salvation issue and what's not a salvation issue, year after year, and generation after generation, but those arguments become coping mechanisms for dealing with what we're really talking about. With Jesus, we're not talking about what worship practices may change our eternal status before God. We're talking about worship, in Spirit and in truth, worship that understands the salvation that is happening all around us if we will but uncross our arms and open our eyes.

Apparently the woman was transformed when she looked across the relational and social chasms and saw that God really just wanted her heart. She was beginning to understand that believing in Jesus is about reconciliation of those who are estranged and that he is about inclusion rather than exclusion, that the Spirit dwells in both Samaritan and Jewish worshipers, and that the Spirit dwells in both men and women. Salvation is ethnically, gender, and socially inclusive.

A marginalized Samaritan woman became a witness to her village. She gave testimony about the Savior of the world. Jesus probably made his followers more uncomfortable than they already were on their sojourn through Samaria, because the text says that when they returned from their food expedition, they were surprised to find him talking with a woman. Imagine how surprised and uncomfortable they were when they found out they would stay for two more days and follow up on her missionary work in the village! Jesus taught his original disciples not to worship their own comfort. He modeled for them what the real salvation issues are, and as disciples today, we still have to learn what that means.

With an understanding of what has been done in our lives because of Jesus Christ, we are called to testify with a marginalized Samaritan woman that the time has come to worship in Spirit and in truth. Some may be uncomfortable by the fullness of inclusion brought through Jesus, but like the Samaritan woman, we may be transformed. We may be set free by it. The message of the cross is foolishness to those who are perishing, but to us who are being saved, it is the power of God.

My friend Marnie said to me recently, "I'm not sure how it happened, but in the past few years, I have let go of the fear that was instilled in me about worship. I've stopped thinking about what makes me comfortable or uncomfortable. I've come to realize that God wants my heart to be pure and my worship to be real more than I am to figure it all out and get it all right." With my friend, I honor God's desire for our worship. It's time to throw off the fear that hinders us and trust the Spirit who dwells in every believer. Bob Randolph of the Brookline, Massachusetts, Church of Christ has written, " . . . women will preach in Churches of Christ when we decide not to be afraid. We live in a dangerous world, with many things to be fearful about, but I believe that our God has better things in mind for us than fear."

When comfort in worship is worshiped more than God is worshiped, it is time for us to uncross our arms, step back from our doctrinal arguments, let go of our fear, and consider what it means to worship in Spirit and in truth.

I know it's uncomfortable for some Christians in my fellowship to hear me—or any other woman—preach, but we must discuss what's really at stake. The stakes are not about whether or not women preach on a Sunday morning. The stakes are higher than that. We're talking about how we participate in the salvation of God as a community. It's what was at stake with the woman at the well as she opened her eyes and with the disciples as they opened their eyes. It's at stake for us as we open our eyes every Sunday. I want those who get stuck on the idea that women are to be silent to consider what what they are saying no to—not to one issue on a list of potential salvation issues like whose cups we drink out of or on whose mountain we worship, but the larger picture of salvation.

The best story we can ever tell is the one that woman told in Samaria when she got so excited that she left her water jar behind at the well (I love that little detail). She left behind *water*, and she ran to talk about living water, salvation that radically welcomes and includes and makes room for all at the table of the Lord.

My life calling is to join that Samaritan woman in proclaiming Jesus Christ the Messiah. I proclaim Christ because I hope to hear it said, "We no longer believe just because of what you said; now we have heard for ourselves, and we know that this man really is the Savior of the world" (John 4:42).

Recently I missed a phone call from my husband, but he left a message. I dialed my voicemail, and I heard a crackly message that meant he was holding his phone up to the radio speaker in the car while he was driving. He was singing along with Randy Travis, "My love is deeper than the holler . . . and longer than the call of the whippoorwill." John learned to love my song—he even learned to play it on his guitar—nothing short of miraculous when it comes to his longstanding disdain for twangy country music, his personal musical preferences, and comfortable choices. It's corny and sappy and probably embarrassing to him that I'm telling our story. But that's how we show that we love each other—we learn to think outside ourselves in order to love the other more.

Radically, the church is called to welcome and make room for the other person. That means learning new things we wouldn't learn if left on our own. It means loving people we wouldn't love if left to our own preferences. It means taking up a cross that is far from comfortable instead of choosing to avoid discomfort. We're not to be people who cross our arms and bring out checklists that make us feel superior about who's in and who's out. We have to do what Jesus told his disciples to do in John 4:35: "Open your eyes and look at the fields! They are ripe for harvest . . . . [T]he sower and the reaper may be glad together."

That is our salvation issue.

chapter twelve | **bodies and the body**

After we lived outside the United States for eight years, it was quite a transition when we returned. Reverse culture shock upon our return was harder for me than the initial culture shock when we first moved to Uganda. We had left in our mid-twenties when our son Nate was just months old, and our daughter Brynn was born on the African continent. We returned to a very different stage of life than when we had left. We hadn't owned a house or sent kids off to school on a school bus. Having been church planters, we had never searched for an existing congregation. Our kids had never lived through the cycle of the four changing seasons. Adjustments were new every morning.

Shopping was perhaps the hardest adjustment for me. The first week we were back, we were staying with friends, and I offered to help with chores around the house. My host gave me the task of going to the grocery store and a list of things to purchase. That didn't sound too hard. I went to Meijer, Michigan's version of Super Wal-Mart, and the first item on the list was *bread*. Simple enough: bread, a standard staple. When I got to the bread aisle, however, I had a moment of culture shock. In Uganda I bought Tip Top Bread, the only choice, for eight years without giving it much thought, and I hadn't thought about whole grain bread, multigrain bread, wheat bread, potato bread, rye bread, Hawaiian bread, lite bread, sourdough bread, Sara Lee, Aunt Millie's, Nature's Own, and Wonder Bread. Not only the wide choice but also the wide gap between poverty and plenty in the world made me dizzy. The bread aisle was a moment of significant reverse culture shock, and there were many. I went back to my host, a shopping basket case.

Perhaps the most significant moments of reverse culture shock came later, however, when I finally accomplished the grocery store task and made it to the checkout aisle. As I stood in line, the barrage of images and messages about women's bodies on magazine covers almost knocked me over. It's not that I hadn't seen a magazine in eight years, but part of reverse culture shock is resistance to what constitutes a culture. It's impossible to ignore the fact that in our culture our bodies are central, even idolized: pecs, abs, breasts, buns, shiny faces, dry hair, oily hair, how to make your body different, how to make your partner's body feel good, and whether or not famous people have good or bad bodies. I'm not criticizing an emphasis upon being healthy, but the primary message of magazines at the grocery checkout is not health. It's an unhealthy focus on our bodies. People become objects when we see them in a way that's disconnected from holistic life.

Images of bodies surround us: TV, billboards, magazines, newspapers. We're used to it, for the most part, and at some point, we have to discuss it with our kids. I tell mine that magazines reflect the world's view, not the Christian view. Despite what our culture tells us, our bodies are not all about biology. Our bodies and our sexuality are aspects of being human, very good ones, but not the only ones.

I recently found out that I've made my point clear to Brynn. As we drove by a Hooters restaurant, where the most noticeable attribute of the servers is not necessarily their serving skills, Brynn said, "Hey Mom, you know what would be fun? Let's go in Hooters, and you can do your objectification of women rant."

The scriptural narrative makes it clear that God wants *all* of who we are; we are to love with our heart, soul, mind, and strength. With God, our bodies are not to be objectified, but be temples filled with the Holy Spirit. Joining the kingdom of God means that we join in God's redemption of all that we see now and all that we anticipate knowing more fully, and we look at everything differently through the eyes of people who understand redemption holistically.

As the magazines and the Hooters restaurants make clear, we live in a society that objectifies women. There's a loud cultural voice shouting that certain women are valued above others, based solely on their physical features. The loud voice advocates an ideal found in everything from a particular kind of cheekbones to a certain size jeans to skin and hair that meet an ideal standard. When our daughters realize they cannot meet that ideal, they turn to physical mutilation, anorexia, bulimia, low self-esteem, over-exercising, cutting, sexual experimentation at younger and younger ages, and attraction to the wrong kind of men. They undergo surgery on their bodies at younger and younger ages to get closer to the ideal they see in fashion magazines and on TV. Women like me look at our own bodies as we age, and we are disappointed when we *look* forty or when we *look* fifty. Tragically, we fail to see our whole being through God's eyes.

Imagine how it sounds to those in areas of the world where there is a lack of food that Western culture suffers anxiety about weight, dieting, and exercise. No other culture suffers on this level: According to the National Association of Anorexia Nervosa and Associated Disorders, up to twenty-four million people in the United States of all ages and genders suffer from an eating disorder (anorexia, bulimia, and binge eating disorder). Anorexia is the third most common chronic illness among adolescents. Approximately 50 percent of adolescents and young women between fifth and twelfth grades are trying to lose weight, even though most are already at or below normal weight. Eighty-one percent of ten-year-old girls report that they are afraid of being fat. All of this occurs even though the reality is that the body type portrayed as the ideal in advertising is possessed naturally by only 5 percent of American females. Our obsession with the "ideal" female body borders on insanity. We don't need an objective alien to come to our grocery store checkout lines to tell us that.

There's no doubt that body image confusion exists for women in our culture. To further confuse us, at the same time that our society objectifies women with a loud voice about the ideal body, another voice says that women can achieve anything they want to achieve, and that women contribute more to society than attractive bodies. Women's rights activist Elizabeth Cady Stanton said, "I would have girls regard themselves not as adjectives but as nouns." Women like Hillary Rodham Clinton, Madeleine Albright, Margaret Thatcher, and Condoleezza Rice deserve our admiration and thanks because their lives shout that women may be defined as nouns like leader, politician, role model, professor, debater, scholar, arbiter, peacemaker, and speechmaker. Women hold high rank in the military, and they are CEOs in some of our most successful companies. They are teachers, superintendents, doctors, lawyers, scientists, social workers, and bank executives. In 2011, three women, Ellen J. Sirleaf, Leymah Gbowee, and Tawakkol Karman literally led the world to see all women more clearly and were jointly awarded the Nobel Peace Prize *"for their non-violent struggle for the safety of women and for women's rights to full participation in peacebuilding work."* We tell every little boy *and girl* that they can be anything, any *noun* they want to be. This message represents a significant voice in our world, advice that counters objectification of women.

The problem, I think, is that we in the church have a hard time bringing two cultural messages about women together into the holistic gospel. I remember the cheer we yelled in our little basketball gymnasium at

Melbourne High School: "We've got the spirit, yes we do. We've got the spirit, how about you?" The opposing team would shout their cheer back at us, "*We've* got the spirit, yes *we* do." Each side shouted back and forth at each other, clamoring to be the loudest, and from my position on the free-throw line of the basketball court, I couldn't hear anything because of all the noise coming at me from every side.

Our daughters are in the middle of a metaphoric basketball court, with two messages being shouted at them. It's a confusing, overwhelming place to be. No amount of covering her ears can block out the shouting match. One side says, "Your body is how you will be measured as a person." It's an alluring message, and our world shouts it loudly. The other side says, "Define yourself with your grades and intelligence. Be a leader in a world that needs leaders." This message of empowerment for women, while important, is not primarily how I hope our daughters will define themselves. They are wonderful, God's beloved children, whether they make all As or all Fs. They are important whether or not they succeed according to this world's definition of success.

As a woman who is not exempt from this battle, I can tell you that on any given day or any given moment in a woman's life, one side or the other will be winning the battle. As a shouting match about body parts goes on in our culture, it can seem that our daughters cannot hear the Christian message above all the clatter, or that, in the worst cases, there is no Christian message for our daughters to hear.

The Christian message should be that God values our whole being. God wants all of us, not just our brains, not just our physical bodies, not just our souls apart from all the rest. The kingdom perspective is that God is reconciling all of who we are. As the church, we must consider what we want to teach our daughters regarding their identity as women from a Christian perspective, and we have to make that message more appealing and more significant than the worldly alternatives.

Luke's Gospel contains a couple of thought-provoking lines that speak to the physical bodies of women in tension with their understanding of identity through faith. In the first century, there weren't *Cosmopolitan* magazines at the local markets, but women were defined physically, and giving birth to children was inseparable from a women's identity (as it is today). In Luke 1, Mary went to visit Elizabeth while they were both pregnant. Luke tells us that when Elizabeth heard Mary's greeting, her child leaped within her, and she was filled with the Holy Spirit. She said to Mary:

> Blessed are you among women, and blessed is the fruit of your womb. And why has this happened to me, that the mother of my Lord comes to me? For as soon as I heard the sound of your greeting, the child in my womb leaped for joy. And blessed is she who believed that there would be a fulfillment of what was spoken to her by the Lord. (Luke 1:41–45 NRSV)

Elizabeth blessed Mary twofold. In essence, she declared: You are blessed because of your womb, and you are blessed for your faith. It's a beautiful scene. I imagine that in the dramatic circumstances of her young life, Mary was in need of a blessing. Elizabeth's words must have powerfully blessed Mary as she lived with the physical and spiritual realities of her situation.

Later in Luke's story, chapter 11, however, I think we see clarification of Elizabeth's blessing when Jesus seemed to make a point in how he chose to quote (or not quote) her. Notice the exchange that took place between Jesus and a woman in the crowd after Jesus cast a demon out of a man.

Because of the miracle, some in the crowd were amazed, but others suggested he was in league with he-who-must-not-be-named, a general meaning of the term "Beelzebul." Jesus told his critics that unless God came to live in them, they would remain vulnerable to devastation, as they had seen before in the history of Israel. So Jesus took their discussion and expanded it into a lesson for the community of Israel as a whole.

The crowd watched in admiration as Jesus rose to the challenge with authoritative teaching.

> As Jesus was saying these things, a woman in the crowd called out, "Blessed is the mother who gave you birth and nursed you." He replied, "Blessed rather are those who hear the word of God and obey it." (Luke 11:27–28)

Sometimes I think we forget that the crowds were just as amazed by the way Jesus taught with authority as they were with the miracles. N. T. Wright notes that one woman in the crowd, caught up in the exchange, so admired the authoritative response Jesus gave that she shouted something like, "Imagine what it must be like to be the mother of this impressive man." Jesus turned to her and said, "When we talk about the Word of God, make sure there's obedience, not mere applause, for hearing and obeying are far more important than anything else."

Notice Jesus' teaching—blessing comes not when a woman's body performs one of its biological functions, it comes because one believes and lives accordingly. I don't think Jesus was being disrespectful toward his mother, Elizabeth, or the woman in the crowd. I think he wanted to emphasize that hearing and obeying God's Word are primary. Jesus must have had his reasons for making that clarification. Could it be that while some women may or may not be blessed by the world's standard of physical or cultural success, all women may be blessed spiritually?

This view of blessing applies to women and men alike. We are blessed if we hear the Word of God and follow it. It's admirable if a person is outwardly beautiful or handsome. It's a blessing when a woman can give birth to children or a man can father sons and daughters. It's wonderful when a noble wife meets the standards of the Proverbs 31 woman or when a godly husband provides for his family. It's important when women and men make meaningful contributions in secular work settings.

But Jesus seems to say, "It's a blessing that my mother gave birth to me and nurtured me, but the real blessing comes to those who imitate her when they hear the word of God and obey it." I love it when people tell me I'm a good mother, a good wife, and a good teacher. Those are important, valued aspects of my being. But I'm longing to hear from my church—blessed are you because you hear the will of God and follow it. I want to be a fully expressed woman, not an isolated individual. I want to be a participant in an interdependent life. I think it's our task today to function together in such a way that every child of God may hear and obey God's Word. I want to be a part of a church like that—and so do other women in our culture.

Paul expanded on the idea of how we go about helping one another hear and obey. He used the image of the body to explain how this can work, developing the idea of the body in several of his letters.

In Paul's time, Michelle Lee writes, the body was used as a metaphor for the power of the Roman Empire, with the sovereign as the head and the provinces as the members, sending a message to common people to submit to the head for the good of everyone. Seneca, a first-century Roman philosopher, made the point that when people protect the head, they in essence protect themselves. Seneca suggested that the head, the sovereign, is the source of life and breath to the body, the commonwealth. He argued that the sovereign should be merciful because that's what best serves his self-interest in a unified empire. The body image was widely understood as a mechanism for keeping people within their own social structure and place in society.

Paul redefined that image in terms of the Christian perspective, and in doing so, he re-imagined power through the example of Jesus Christ. Paul didn't just talk about *a body*, but about the body of Christ himself, reminding his readers that the head of the body *died* for all the other members of the body. What a contrast to the cultural understanding of a head that has the power to crush those who do not submit to power! Paul described a body in which all the members of the body are interdependent, in submission to and following the example of a head who gave up his power and died for them. Paul especially emphasized the equal value of weaker members.

Gordon Fee points out that Paul made it clear that all members are necessary if there is to be a body. Paul taught that life as a body—unity in diversity—is the only way a church can function. It's about power as defined by the head, who is Christ, dying for all the rest. It's when love triumphs in the body, that God's people will be known to the world around them and the good news of Jesus will be proclaimed. Without love, Paul seemed to say, gifts don't matter. Love is the only context for gifts, or anything else in the Christian life.

When Paul emphasized the triumph of love in the body, he wanted Christians in Corinth, for example, to grasp their corporate identity with Christ as their head. He was saying that they shouldn't just change their external, physical behavior as a means of self service. Rather, he taught that they should think of each other as interdependent members working in tandem for the gospel rather than for self-serving, individual means. They can understand what that means only when they learn to see power as identified through a crucified Christ who emptied himself of power.

Paul described the body metaphor in a culturally appropriate way in a specific time and place. Now it's time for us to look at our culture and seek to understand how we can most effectively function as a body in our time and place. Paul makes it clear to us that believers are in a horizontal relationship with one another, and we have obligations to each other. The church, with all our mutually interdependent parts, is ultimately one body. Just like the human body, the church will have many parts, all with different functions. Church members will have different gifts (1 Cor. 12:14–16), but despite those differences, they will function as one because that's God's design (v. 18). Just as it's illogical to think of any part of the human body being unnecessary in a physical body, it's true in the church as well. The members of the body of Christ should rejoice together (v. 26), no person should be considered inferior or unwanted (v. 16), and no one should be excluded because some members are superior to others (v. 21). Parts of the body that seem to be weak should be seen as vital (vv. 22–24) because all are important to God. Interdependence, immersed in love, is the theme of Paul's advice to the Corinthians.

Now let me present questions about today, specifically churches in Western society. How are we to relate to one another in submission to the head and function as a body whose interdependence empowers every member to obey God's Word? What message do we want to give every female member and every male member about their places in the body? Is it fathomable that the culture today requires us to make a place for women, even if that wouldn't have been culturally feasible in the first century?

Women today may lead in virtually any role outside the church. Although there is more progress to be made, we currently experience a growing amount of openness to the leadership of women in our society. Churches that limit the participation of women in leadership must grapple with this question: In light of our current culture, would some say that our stance on gender distinctions thwarts our interdependent possibilities as a whole body?

In a recent article titled "The Newest U.S. Mission Field: Women" in a *Christianity Today* online blog by Sharon H. Miller, Miller cites evidence gathered by George Barna showing that since 1991, the overall number of women attending church dropped eleven percentage points, down to 44 percent. She also points out declines in Bible reading among women and significant decline in Sunday school involvement and volunteer activities. The study cited indicates that the "only religious behavior that increased among women in the last twenty years was becoming unchurched. That rose a startling seventeen percentage points—among the largest drops in church attachment identified in the research." The number of unchurched men also increased, but only by 9 percent.

Miller acknowledges the complexity of these gender fluctuations and nuances, but she says they undoubtedly show that our culture is shifting and that churches are adjusting to the cultural shifts. With the number of women surpassing the number of men obtaining advanced degrees, and with a growing percentage of women entering the labor force, Miller challenges Christians to ask how we should be reaching out to our communities, particularly educated and professional women:

> Christian women must be able to articulate what they believe and why. How is the church equipping women for this? Are Christian women able to answer the basic theological questions of their neighbors, co-workers, and friends? And as more American women populate the workplace, how is the church supporting the Christian women in their midst? Are churches training women as effective missionaries in their fields of expertise? Finally, is the church a welcome place to this new generation of educated, professional women? How might a newly converted, female CEO find her gifts expressed in an evangelical church? How might a woman with financial savvy or her own law practice be able to serve her local congregation? Will these women be welcomed as resources, or ignored and untapped? Churches have the choice between investing or burying the talents

of these capable sisters; women are less likely to attend a church in which the latter is the norm.

This article weighs in on a discussion that is confusing at best and offensive at worst to many women in our culture at large when they enter a church and it is male dominated. The gospel is not proclaimed in their lives; instead it is hindered. Sometimes I think we get so comfortable with what we're comfortable with in church that we are more concerned about staying comfortable than with advancing the gospel of our Lord Jesus Christ. It's easy to continue believing what we've always been taught about the role of women in church ministries if we meet together in our little holy huddles (which are by all accounts becoming smaller and smaller huddles), but it becomes difficult to believe what we've always been taught when we attempt to engage the gospel with the real people who live outside those huddles. If we expect women of our culture to join interdependent body life, then we must consider how Paul's words speak to us today, because we are the body of Christ, and each of us is a part of it.

I believe that when we refuse to allow women to participate in our church leadership because they are women, perhaps denying them participation because of their female anatomy rather than their minds, hearts, and spiritual gifts, we are joining the wrong side of the cultural shouting match around us. We are joining the side that objectifies women.

Admittedly, important points of the gospel will never make sense in our culture, and they should not be lost. I'm not advocating that we should water down the gospel. The major tenets of our faith must not be lost. For example, suffering as the way to the cross must be held high regardless of cultural situations in which suffering is equated with shame. Another major tenet that must not be lost is an understanding of sin. Sin as a human condition must be confessed in the light of the blood of

Jesus, regardless of how unpopular it is to call a sin a sin. Additionally, life through Jesus Christ must be held as the way, the truth, and the life, regardless of a pluralistic culture that welcomes many ways to God.

Central truths of the gospel must not be lost, but the issue of women's participation in church ministries cannot be a test of who is saved and who is not, about which group of people is saved and which is not. I just don't see that in the scriptural narrative. If the command "Women are to be silent in the church" is really at the center of the gospel, then I will submit to it because what's at the center is that on which we stake our lives.

The place of women in God's story, starting just after the fall (when renewal of creation became necessary), follows a trajectory in which God is redeeming all creation, including a place for *all humanity* at the table of the Lord who came to redeem our brokenness. That's why Paul redefined the image of the body in line with the reality of the perfection of relationships in heaven. Until perfection comes, we live in that trajectory, which I believe means that *all* of humanity is invited to *full* participation in the broken-and-yet-healed interdependent body of Jesus. It's a mystery that this body can be broken and healed at the same time, but that's the mystery in which we live. We grow and change as we work toward a functioning body. As situations arise, as they did in Corinth, the church must address challenges within the local context, consider gospel-threatening issues that are at stake, and function as the dynamic body of Christ, full of members who are interdependent with one another.

Might we ask whether we are currently working for the curse (Gen. 3:16) or for the cross (Gen. 3:28)? The body metaphor in 1 Corinthians 12 is about gifts that are not given based on gender but are given for the common good; aren't these points relevant to the inclusion of women throughout church life? There is disagreement on the role of women in church ministries, but my plea is that we consider the possibility that the canon of Scripture points to a church that is on a path toward openness for all, to a narrative that gives an equal place to every son *and daughter* of God. Because the coming age is not yet reality, we live in ongoing tension with change. Good news is about the new thing that is coming. That's what news is! There was tension in that news for Paul, and there will be tension for us, but we must embrace the journey interdependently for the sake of the gospel.

The church is to be a unique, dynamic community where spiritual gifts are the basis of relationship and connection to one another. Scripture must be considered in light of culture, looking at the big story seen in the whole canon, rather than taking commands out of context and applying them for all times and places. It's hard work, this process. It's impossible without the guidance of the Holy Spirit and without the discerning process of the whole interdependent body of Christ, seeking, learning, growing, and reaching for understanding together.

Women in our Western world today desperately need to know that they are worth far more than the sum of their body parts. They need to hear that message from the church. The church must rise above the clamor of voices in our world and help our daughters define themselves, not by the confusing messages of our world but by the interdependent identity that's offered through the church. The church of today, like the church of Paul's day, must redefine the term *body image* for the sake of the body of Christ.

Our culture desperately needs a church that acknowledges women as full human beings, made in God's image, a safe haven where women are not objectified. We need a church that equips women for leadership in a world that needs leaders. Our culture desperately needs the church to voice the truth that all human beings bear God's image and must be valued above the illusions of this world. We need a church that embodies power as Christ defined power when he gave it up for the sake of others. I refuse to be a mother who doesn't see all that God has created my daughter and son to be. It is my deep plea that each reader of this book will make a prayerful decision to raise a voice in his or her corner of the world that will overcome the marginalization of women that's occurred in society and been sanctioned by local churches.

chapter thirteen | **working and waiting**

—When I visited Westminster Abbey in London, I was awestruck. It embodies the good and bad of nearly one thousand years of history, history in brick and mortar. It's a place of worship. It's a work of art. It's a cemetery. It's a museum. It's a story of priorities. With a presence that is stately, solid, and commanding, there's also something about the abbey's history that is still in process, with new possibilities in each generation.

There's a subway exit (mind the gap) not far from the abbey, so when I visited, I emerged from speedy underground transportation with hordes of fellow travelers, and we entered the hustle and bustle of London life. In the distance was the monstrous London Eye Ferris wheel going around, taking tourists to a view of London from on high. If one wanted a Starbucks coffee, she might swing by the one on Victoria Street on her way to the abbey and grab a cup to go. London is moving. London is busy. London is modern.

And then, there's Westminster Abbey.

All the rushing, all the hurry and haste stand in contrast to the experience of the abbey. I'm sure some tourists rush through, in one door and out the other, glancing at the beautiful ceiling along the way, headed to the Hard Rock Café London for a red, white, and blue burger.

But there's something so very wrong about a sense of urgency in this cathedral. Westminster Abbey stands in the middle of the rush, serene and stately, as an invitation to pause, breathe, and reflect.

Jean Gimpel wrote a book titled *The Cathedral Builders* in which he describes the medieval mindset of people who undertook building a cathedral without steel, cranes, backhoes, or dump trucks. Stone, light, and human toil were their resources, and that stone, light, and humanity would point toward God.

History is replete with kings, cardinals, and abbots who oversaw the building of medieval cathedrals. Some did so with deep faith and honorable, worshipful intentions. Some did so as an exercise of power, arrogance, and control. I think of the lesser-credited master masons and builders who literally spent their lives on the building sites of cathedrals. Henry of Reyns is credited as the earliest architect of Westminster Abbey, working as master architect for King Henry III as the project began in 1245. There's evidence Reyns had visited cathedrals in France for inspiration, and then I imagine him envisioning the structure that would become Westminster Cathedral, designing in his mind what would be the highest Gothic vault in England, planning to accentuate the height with narrow aisles that would be his own design. He may have visited Dorset and chosen blocks of Purbeck marble that would serve as columns for the feat of architecture he had in mind.

The abbey was not completed in the lifetimes of Henry III and Henry of Reyns. They didn't expect that it would. The sheer magnitude of the design would demand lifetimes of work for kings, cardinals, masons, builders, and common laborers, so they started something they knew would take hundreds and hundreds of years to complete. Only one nave had been completed by the time Henry III died.

Through the years, there were stops and starts, triumphs and failures. But along the way, work continued on the cathedral, and it is clear in the architectural unity of the abbey that the original design of Henry III's masons was followed. Henry V and Henry VII added chapels, along with the delicately carved fan-vaulted ceiling. All those years of work created Westminster Abbey, considered one of the most perfect buildings ever erected in England.

All these names and dates are distant history now when visitors walk through the abbey and admire its beauty, but imagine the masons and builders who spent their entire lives contributing to its construction. Men apprenticed their sons who apprenticed their sons who apprenticed their sons, and through all their work and time and patience, the abbey became an awe-inspiring combination of stone and light that points to God.

Leaving the fast-paced world of twenty-first century London, with our Western demand for immediate results, and entering the historical abbey, it struck me that medieval kings and their working-class subjects were willing to contribute to something whose end they knew they would never see. They saw value in contributing toward the creation of the abbey because they could see how their unique contributions (moving marble from Dorset to London or setting rubies and sapphires into the stained-glass windows) would contribute in pointing toward God.

Those patient cathedral builders knew something about eternity that we modern, obsessively hurried, impatient Christians need to learn. They knew how to work in their moment of time without forgetting to honor both the past and the future.

Past, present, and future—that's the epic story where I've made sense of my own story. It's where I find my present calling. I'm like one of those laborers in the cathedral, making my lifetime contribution to the creation of something I will not see completed in this lifetime. I'm a part of something that was before me, is now, and will be brought to completion in some way I don't fully understand. I simply know there's a calling for believers to contribute; there's a calling for me to do my part.

Back to Westminster Abbey. As I left the abbey and reentered the sights and sounds of London, I turned around and looked back at the inspiring cathedral. We exited from a different gate than we entered, and I was looking at the west gate. As my gaze progressed along the outside contours of the Gothic structure, my observation halted in surprise as I saw a statue of someone I recognized immediately, Dr. Martin Luther King Jr. I would not have expected Dr. King to show up on a niche in the west gate of Westminster Abbey in England, and yet the sculpture blended in and looked like it had been there for hundreds of years. I was intrigued.

I learned that in 1998, ten twentieth-century martyrs were commemorated with statues as an addition to Westminster Abbey. The martyrs chosen by the abbey represent religious persecution and oppression from every continent. They died for their faith and beliefs, victims of Nazism, racism, communism, and religious persecution. Upon closer inspection, I saw others whose stories I knew: German theologian Dietrich Bonhoeffer, whose ideology centered on peace and nonviolence, but he was ultimately hanged by the Nazis. I saw Janani Luwum, who was assassinated in Uganda during the rule of Idi Amin for being an outspoken Anglican archbishop. There was Manche Masemola, a young South African woman who sought to join the Anglican Church against her parents' wishes and died as a result of their beatings in 1928 at the age of 16.

While it surprised me initially, the addition of twentieth-century martyrs to Westminster Abbey honors the highest ideals of the abbey, stone and light and human toil pointing to God. When the early builders died, leaving the abbey incomplete, they trusted the next generation to continue, with hope that the original design would be followed.

Past, present, and future—that's where I've made sense of my story, and really it is *our* story. We are like those laborers on the building site, making our lifetime contributions to the creation of something new we may not see completed in this lifetime. We're a part of something that was before us, is now, and will be brought to completion in some way we don't fully understand. God is the master architect; Jesus is the foundation. There's a calling for believers to contribute, to use good materials, and to build wisely and in a way appropriate to the foundation, which is Jesus Christ. We follow the apostle Paul:

> According to the grace of God given to me, like a skilled master builder I laid a foundation, and someone else is building on it. Each builder must choose with care how to build on it. For no one can lay any foundation other than the one that has been laid; that foundation is Jesus Christ. Now if anyone builds on the foundation with gold, silver, precious stones, wood, hay, straw—the work of each builder will become visible, for the Day will disclose it, because it will be revealed with fire, and the fire will test what sort of work each has done. If what has been built on the foundation survives, the builder will receive a reward. If the work is burned, the builder will suffer loss; the builder will be saved, but only as through fire. (1 Cor. 3:10–15)

On this foundation, I find my calling to do my part, proactively, wisely, and humbly. I see my place as I join God in the new creation going on in our world. God set about a process of redemption of shattered creation, and we're in one place and time along the timeline of that process. We should expect to see movement. Contributing to new creation should not simply imply a reversion to a fixed and unchanging reality. It should rather call us to a recommitment to the original project God has been leading all along, a project that calls us to contribute, build, and develop as time goes on, always expecting new and exciting developments.

Believers are called to join the ongoing process of what God is doing, what God is building, what God is redeeming, what God is saving, what God is setting right. We should expect to see the kingdom more fully coming on earth as it is in heaven, and it's my conviction that the kingdom Jesus proclaimed is one that continually works toward and anticipates the full inclusion of all who confess his name.

As our foundation, Jesus is our peace who destroyed barriers and dividing walls, creating one humanity, bringing peace and reconciliation. Like the fractures between Jews and Gentiles, divisions between male and female are being made whole.

> Consequently, you are no longer foreigners and aliens, but fellow citizens with God's people and members of God's household, built on the foundation of the apostles and prophets, with Christ Jesus himself as the chief cornerstone. In him the whole building is joined together and rises to become a holy temple in the Lord. And in him you too are being built together to become a dwelling in which God lives by his Spirit. (Eph. 2:19–22)

I want a role. I want a job. I may not see the final cathedral in this lifetime, but give me a shovel. Let me dig a ditch. Let me design a window through which the morning sun will shine. Or let me pray words of blessing over those who are climbing dangerously high to build the nave. Let us continually consult the master architect so that we may be unified as we renovate from generation to generation.

This work of joining new creation is no easier than building a cathedral that took a thousand years. It's hard work to live in a community that is to embody power as revealed on a cross. It's hard work to resist temptation for dominance and independence. Yet when we have eyes to see, we are given glimpses of oneness in Christ that remind us what's coming, and we each do our part with the hope of what will be the full reality one day.

What if Henry of 1245 could visit the abbey of 2012? Would he be impressed? Would he even recognize it? Would he be disappointed in any element of variance from the original design? Would he sit, awestruck, in Poet's Corner and ask to be told the continuing story of the cathedral that began so long ago? One thing I am certain he would know is that he did not make that cathedral happen alone.

"There are two things we cannot do alone," said Paul Tournier. "One is to be married and the other is to be a Christian." As a believer, as I have stepped into God's big story, I have at times been tempted to "go it alone." Like Eve, the temptation of being independent sounds much easier than being dependent on others who don't do things the way I want or see things the way I do or interpret scriptures the way I think is correct.

No church I know of gets it all right, and no person gets it all right, certainly not me. I'm part of something that is being made right. I believe that when this creation is fully made right, all will be heirs in Christ. All will be one in Christ. For now, I seek to be a part of a community that defines our relationships in anticipation of that oneness. I want a community that makes a place for Amy McLaughlin, who wrote to me recently after she delivered a sermon in a preaching class with Dr. David Fleer at Lipscomb University. She describes the standing ovation given to her by her classmates, her professor, and her parents, who flew to Nashville specifically to hear the capstone sermon for the course:

> I was overwhelmed. I wanted to run off the stage and join them in applauding for the message God delivered. I looked back at my parents, who were both crying, and then back at Dr. Fleer, whose eyes were clearly watering. Dr. Fleer was beyond gracious in his compliments, and my peers were

far too kind. One of my male peers commented on how the message was exactly what he needed to hear. I felt so blessed and humbled that God would be willing to speak through me! So, I said, "All right, Dr. Fleer, I'm ready for my critique. Lay it on me." He responded, "Amy, I am not going to critique you. I do not want to distract you from this moment. Class, we just witnessed Amy stumbling upon her calling. Amy, go sit down and think about what we've said, and never forget this moment for the rest of your life." Needless to say, that moment was a dramatic turning point for me. I have no idea what the future holds, but I'm still excited that God is willing to use me. I'm planning to stay within the Churches of Christ (if none of us stay, nothing will change).

I want a community that makes a place for Amy, a community that makes a place for Maggie, who wants to pass the communion tray, and Abby, who is called to lead worship, and Poem, who wants to preach, for they are heirs in Christ, daughters with jobs to do in God's new world, here and now.

When the old order has passed away and everything is even newer in a way we can't imagine, it is my conviction that male and female will be full heirs according to Christ. So, I believe we should join God in living into that vision as fully as possible in our time and place, honoring the past but looking forward to the future.

And I heard a loud voice from the throne saying, "Look! God's dwelling place is now among the people, and he will dwell with them. They will be his people, and God himself will be with them and be their God. He will wipe every tear from their eyes. There will be no more death or mourning or crying or pain, for the old order of things has passed away."

He who was seated on the throne said, "I am making everything new!" Then he said, "Write this down, for these words are trustworthy and true." (Rev. 21:3–5)

In the meantime, we work, and we wait.

Together.

afterword

My paternal grandmother, Mildred Gaston, died before
I was born of an invasive brain tumor. I've heard stories and know about
her from my dad and others who knew her. At one time in my life, just
before John and I moved to Uganda, Daddy said to me, "I wish my mother
could have known you—you're a lot like her. She loved God so much, and
she would have been proud of you for being a missionary."

I stare into those old black and white photographs, trying to see who
she was. I see a nose, a chin, and a forehead I recognize in my cousins and
in myself. But I don't really know all that it means to be like her or to make
her proud. Don't we all need that from our parents and grandparents, no
matter how old we are?

Last year I visited my Aunt Connie, and she made my favorite chocolate meringue pie. It's been my favorite for a long time, and Aunt Connie
always remembers everybody's favorites. Since I've lived far from home
all my adult life, I get special treatment every time I go home, so I often
get chocolate pie. On that particular day, in Aunt Connie's kitchen, I saw
the recipe card she had used when baking the pie, and it said at the top,
"Mildred Gaston's chocolate pie." I hadn't known the pie was originally

my grandmother's recipe, but I liked that it was. I copied the recipe, including the old-timey word "oleo," and took the recipe home with me.

I'm a good cook. My children say it's one of their favorite qualities about me. But I am not good at pies. I gave up several years ago because I can never get the crust quite right. I bake cookies and cakes instead and wait for Aunt Connie to bake the pies.

Still, I became determined to make Mildred Gaston's chocolate pie. Maybe it sounds corny, but it was about much more than baking a pie. It was a way to learn more about who I am. So I got all the ingredients, followed the directions exactly, and called Aunt Connie three times for advice.

The pie was awful. The chocolate was runny. The crust was too brown. The meringue didn't meet the edge of the crust. *Terrible* is not an understatement.

But I'm stubborn. Maybe it comes from Mildred; I don't know. I immediately made another pie. John and our friend Mark were in the house while all this was going on, so they saw the first pie. Then they saw the second pie, almost as bad as the first. Finally, on the third try, my Mildred Gaston pie was edible.

I've made the pie several times since. I'm actually getting good at it—still not as good as Aunt Connie, but I think Mildred would be pleased with the effort, happy that I want to bake her pie. Perhaps she would feel honored by my efforts to be a bit like her.

Sometimes I wish we could see that God is pleased with our efforts. We don't have to get it perfect, and we make messes along the way.

But we're trying.

I wish we could look at each other and see what God sees.

I want to look at my family and neighbors and friends and see that they are trying. The gift we give God and we give one another is that while we keep trying, we learn to look at other people and see that they are trying.

Grace tastes so good.

As I finish writing this book and send it to print, I think I could try even harder and rewrite it a hundred more times, and I would still find words to change: words that might sound kinder, words that might push harder, words that might make a better argument, words that might offend less, words that might more adequately satisfy my academic friends, words that might more clearly explain who I am to those who do not want an academic argument, words that might more fully share what really matters in life.

Words. They are never enough.

But, the true Word, Jesus Christ, is enough.

It's him I hope my story will honor.

author's note

As I've been privileged to spend countless hours in writing this book, I have often been reminded that any challenges I have faced in life are minimal compared to those facing millions of women in the world. If you want to contribute to empowering women who are truly suppressed, please visit http://www.kibogroup.org/projects/womens-empowerment/ and make a donation that will contribute toward the work of empowering my friends in Uganda.

bibliography

"Addressing a crisis of empty pulpits." *The Christian Chronicle,* January 2, 2009. http://www.christianchronicle.org/ article2158647~Addressing_a_crisis_of_empty_pulpits_.

Anderson, Bernhard. *The Unfolding Drama of the Bible.* 4th ed. Minneapolis: Augsburg Fortress, 2006.

Aristotle. *Politics Book 5.* Translated by Horace H. Rackham. Cambridge: Harvard University Press, 1932.

BBC Online Network. "UK: Martyrs of the Modern Era." BBC News, July 9, 1998. http://news.bbc.co.uk/2/hi/uk_news/129587.stm.

Bowman, Craig. "Lecture Notes." Rochester College, MI. December 2011.

Brownson, James. Sp*eaking the Truth in Love: New Testament Resources for a Missional Hermeneutic.* Harrisburg: Trinity Press, 1998.

Chittister, Joan. *Heart of Flesh: A Feminist Spirituality for Women and Men.* Grand Rapids, MI: William B. Eerdmans Publishing Company, 1998.

Donfried, Karl Paul. *The Dynamic Word: New Testament Insights for Contemporary Christians.* New York: HarperCollins, 1981.

Fee, Gordon D. "The Cultural Context of Ephesians 5:18–6:9: Is There A Divinely Ordained Hierarchy in the Life of the Church and Home That is Based on Gender Alone?" *Priscilla Papers* 16.1 (2002): 3.

———. *The First Epistle to the Corinthians (The New International Commentary on the New Testament).* Grand Rapids, MI: William B. Eerdmans Publishing Company, 1st ed. 1987.

———. *The Epistles to the Colossians, to Philemon, and to the Ephesians (New International Commentary on the New Testament).* Grand Rapids, MI: William B. Eerdmans Publishing Company, 2nd ed. 1984.

Flavius, Josephus. *The Jewish War, Volume II: Books 3–4.* Translated by Henry St. John Thackeray. Cambridge: Harvard University Press, 1927.

———. *Jewish Antiquities, Volume VI: 14–15.* Translated by Ralph Marcus and Allen Wikgren. Cambridge: Harvard University Press, 1943.

Gibson, David. "A Literate Church: The state of Catholic Bible study today." *America,* December 8, 2008. http://www.americamagazine.org/content/article.cfm?article_id=11270.

Goheen, Michael. "The Urgency of Reading the Bible as One Story." *Theology Today* 64.4 (2008): 469–483.

Keener, Craig S. *1–2 Corinthians: The New Cambridge Bible Commentary.* New York: Cambridge University Press, 2005.

———. *Paul, Women, and Wives: Marriage and Women's Ministry in the Letters of Paul.* Peabody, MA: Hendrickson, 1992.

King Jr., Martin Luther, and Peter A. Lillback. *Letter from Birmingham Jail.* Bryn Mawr, PA: Providence Forum, 2003.

Lads to Leaders. "Building Godly Leaders for Tomorrow: Terminology." Accessed March 2009. http://www.lads-to-leaders.org/L2L_Terms.shtml.

LaHaye, Tim. *Spirit-Controlled Temperament: The Best-Selling Classic on Who You Are and Who You Can Become.* Carol Stream, IL: Tyndale House Publishers, 1994.

Lee, Michelle V. *Paul, the Stoics, and the Body of Christ.* Cambridge: Cambridge University Press, 2006.

Lewis, C. S. *The Screwtape Letters.* New York: HarperOne, 2001.

McConnon, Aili. "You Are Where You Sit: How to decode the psychology of the morning meeting." *Business Week.* July 23, 2007. http://

www.businessweek.com/print/magazine/content/07_30/b4043082. htm?chan=gl.

McKnight, Scot. *The Blue Parakeet: Rethinking How You Read the Bible.* Grand Rapids: Zondervan, 2008.

Miller, Sharon. "The Newest U.S. Mission Field: Women." *Her.meneutics: the Christianity Today blog for women.* August 9, 2011. http://blog.christianitytoday.com/women/2011/08/ the_newest_us_mission_field_wo.html.

National Association of Anorexia Nervosa and Associated Disorders, Inc. "Eating Disorders Statistics." Accessed February 17, 2011. http://www.anad.org/get-information/about-eating-disorders/ eating-disorders-statistics/.

Nobel Media AB. "Nobel Peace Prize 2011." Accessed January 12, 2012. http://www.nobelprize.org/nobel_prizes/peace/laureates/2011/#.

Newbigin, Lesslie. *The Gospel in a Pluralist Society.* Grand Rapids, MI: William B. Eerdmans Publishing Company, 1989.

Nouwen, Henri J. M. *Life of the Beloved: Spiritual Living in a Secular World.* New York: The Crossroad Publishing Company, 2002.

Osburn, Carroll. *Women in the Church: Reclaiming the Ideal.* Abilene, TX: Abilene Christian University Press, 2001.

Osiek, Carolyn, Margaret Y. MacDonald, and Janet H. Tulloch. *A Woman's Place: House Churches in Earliest Christianity.* Minneapolis: Fortress Press, 2005.

Parks, Ted. "A preacher shortage? Leaders disagree." *The Christian Chronicle.* February 2002. http://www.christianchronicle.org/ article1337008~A_preacher_shortage%3F_Leaders_disagree.

Plutarch: Moralia. Vol. 1. Translated by Frank Cole Babbitt. Cambridge: Harvard University Press, 1927.

Randolph, Robert. "Why Women Should Be Preaching in the Churches of Christ." *Leaven* 11 (2003): 205.

Schmemann, Alexander. *For the Life of the World.* New York: St. Vladimir's Seminary Press, 1973.

Schürer, Emil. *The History of the Jewish People in the Age of Jesus Christ: (175 B.C.–A.D. 135). Vol. III.2.* Revised and edited by Geza Vermes, Fergus Millar, Martin Goodman, and Pamela Vermes. Edinburgh: T & T Clark, 2004.

Sorkin, Aaron. *The West Wing.* "War Crimes." Season 3, episode 5.

Thomas, Gary. *Sacred Marriage: What If God Designed Marriage to Make Us Holy More than to Make Us Happy?* Grand Rapids: Zondervan, 2000.

U.S. Census Bureau. "October is Family History Month." October 4, 2010. http://blogs.census.gov/2010/10/04/october-is-family-history-month/.

Wright, N. T. *Luke for Everyone.* Westminster: John Knox Press, 2001.

——— . *Scripture and the Authority of God: How to Read the Bible Today.* New York: HarperOne, 2011.

——— . *Simply Christian: Why Christianity Makes Sense.* New York: HarperOne, 2010.

additional resources

Allen, C. Leonard. *Distant Voices: Discovering a Forgotten Past for a Changing Church.* Abilene, TX: Abilene Christian University Press, 1993.

Fee, Groothius, and Ronald W. Pierce. *Discovering Biblical Equality: Complementarity Without Hierarchy.* Westmont, IL: Intervarsity Press, 2004.

Grasham, Bill. "The Role of Women in the American Restoration Movement." *Restoration Quarterly* 41.4 (1999): 211–239.

Grenz, Stanley, and Denise M. Kjesbo. *Women in the Church: A Biblical Theology of Women in Ministry.* Downers Grove, IL: InterVarsity Press, 1995.

Grudem, Wayne. "The Myth of Mutual Submission as an Interpretation of Ephesians 5:21." In *Biblical Foundations for Manhood and Womanhood*, edited by Wayne Grudem, 221–232. Wheaton, IL: Crossway Books, 2002.

Johnson, Alan, ed. *How I Changed My Mind about Women in Leadership: Compelling Stories from Prominent Evangelicals.* Grand Rapids: Zondervan, 2010.

Keener, Craig S. *Paul, Women & Wives: Marriage and Women's Ministry in the Letters of Paul.* Peabody, MA: Hendrickson, 1992.

Mathews, Alice P. *Peaching That Speaks to Women.* Grand Rapids: Baker Academic, 2003.

Patzia, Arthur G. *New International Biblical Commentary: Ephesians, Colossians, Philemon.* Peabody, MA: Hendrickson, 1990.

Silvey, Billie, ed. *Trusting Women: The way of women in Churches of Christ.* Orange, CA: New Leaf Books, 2002.

Theissen, Gerd. *The Social Setting of Pauline Christianity: Essays on Corinth.* Philadelphia: Augsburg Fortress Press, 1982.

Volf, Miroslav. *Captive to the Word of God: Engaging the Scriptures for Contemporary Theological Reflection.* Grand Rapids: William B. Eerdmans Publishing Company, 2010.

Watson, Paul. "Are Women to Pray and Prophesy or Are Women to Remain Silent? Some Pastoral Implications of an Exegesis of I Corinthians 14:34–35." *Leaven* 9.3 (2001): 160.

Webb, William. *Slaves, Women, and Homosexuals: Exploring the Hermeneutics of Cultural Analysis.* Downers Grove, IL: InterVarsity Press, 2001.

Wright, N. T. "Women's Service in the Church: The Biblical Basis." A conference paper for the symposium "Men and Women in the Church." St. John's College, Durham, September 4, 2004. http://www.ntwrightpage.com/Wright_Women_Service_Church.htm.